Arthurian Propaganda

Arthurian Propaganda

Le Morte Darthur
as an Historical Ideal of Life

by Elizabeth T. Pochoda

The University of North Carolina Press
Chapel Hill

Manufactured in the United States of America
ISBN 0-8078-1159-9
Library of Congress Catalog Card Number 75-132256
Printed by The Seeman Printery, Inc.

In memory of my teacher and friend
Rosemond Tuve

Contents

Preface

To preface this study with a succinct statement of its thesis would be somewhat misleading. The argument as it emerges in Chapters 2, 3, and 4 is accompanied by hesitations and qualifications even in its final stages. What I have discovered about the nature of the Arthurian story does not admit of conclusive proof despite the amount of textual evidence which can be brought to bear on the problem. What it does offer instead is, I think, a new and compelling way of reading *Le Morte Darthur* as well as other Arthurian pieces; but perhaps this kind of proof is conclusive enough. In lieu of restating the thesis which arises out of my reading of Arthurian legends and Malory in particular, I shall simply point to the problems raised here and indicate the general shape of the conclusions reached.

If we take the word propaganda in its broadest sense, much of Arthurian literature might be said to be a kind of social propaganda. But by the time we reach Malory's version, the direction and nature of the propaganda have diverged so dramatically from that of the romances and chronicles of the twelfth and thirteenth centuries that the story is virtually turned back on itself. The Arthurian romances of Chrétien, for instance, function as a courtly society's advertisements for itself. The ideals and customs glorified here seem to us to exist independent of social or political considerations precisely because the chivalric goal is one of *personal* perfection, the knight's self-realization. The Arthurian social or political structure, when visible in Chrétien, cannot fail to be a model of social cohesion, since its underlying but unexamined assumption is that the ideal of personal perfection is coincidental with social fulfillment. Like the ennobling virtues of courtly love, this chivalric idealism may simply be a convenient veil for darker social truths, but on the surface at least, the twelfth- and thirteenth-century Arthurian romances propose a congruence of ideal and reality, a reassurance that the noble life exists as an ideal and functions in fact—a reassurance that all orders of existence depend upon it for their continuance. Various resurrections or re-creations of the story most often stress in oblique ways the legend's virtues as an establishment myth—a hint of what the perfect society would have been had chivalry really triumphed.

The term "Historical Ideal of Life" which appears in the title comes from Johan Huizinga's essays on cultural history and indicates that the central issue of this study is the phenomenon of literary revival and literary re-creation of a cultural model. The crucial difference between Malory's view of Arthurian society and the story as it appears in the twelfth- and thirteenth-century romances is that while the latter may present Arthurian life and legend as a model for communal identity, they do so implicitly or unconsciously; its exemplary role is *built in*, so to speak, and the romances do not need to acknowledge the presence of this function. I have argued that in Malory's case the Arthurian legend seems to have been revived and re-created out of earlier models as a pure type of cultural ideal. In the body of this study I have raised a number of questions as to the cultural function of such a revival, and the particular suitability of the Arthurian story for this kind of treatment. In addition, I have uncovered a certain ambivalence on Malory's part towards the legendary material which he so "devotedly" resurrected, and much of my discussion of his book centers on the meaning of this ambivalence, the form which it takes, and its reciprocal relationship to the idealization of Arthurian society.

Chapter 1 surveys briefly previous scholarship on Malory, establishing its relevance to this study. I have handled this material separately, because there is almost no need to refer to it later on; and yet it provides a vantage point for viewing the direction in which my analysis of the story has taken me. Although I owe a great deal to the source studies and structural analyses which have made this kind of thematic study possible, my debt is really implicit, as these materials do not directly affect my interpretation of the book. On the other hand, the strictly critical interpretations of Malory have had very little influence on my work, and my disagreement with them after Chapter 1 is, for the most part, a silent one. Chapter 1 also points to the significant gaps in Malory scholarship and suggests fruitful areas for further critical studies of Malory and other aspects of the late medieval literature.

Chapter 2 begins with a lengthy and tentative statement of the thesis. In essence, I have argued here that there is a central paradox in *Le Morte Darthur* which arises from the fact that although Malory initially seems to have designed the Arthurian ideal along the lines of medieval political theory, by doing so he inevitably uncovered much in the Arthurian story which made it unsuitable as an historical ideal of life. The second part of the chapter discusses those aspects of medieval political theory which contribute to the initial structuring of Malory's historical ideal. In Chapters 3 and 4 these political issues and theories reappear in the analysis of each tale, but I have not bothered to duplicate the footnote references because they are all available in Chapter 2. At the end of Chapter 2 I have discussed those elements in the Arthurian story which make it seem highly conducive to political idealization.

Chapter 3 presents the evidence of Malory at work altering the genre, structure, and themes of his sources in Tales I–IV. Arthurian society as an historical ideal of life emerges here; the grounds for its idealization are its supposed fulfillment of the medieval political aspirations discussed in Chapter 2. In Chapter 4 we see how the excessive idealization of Arthurian society in Tales I–IV takes its toll in the last three tales. The first part of the chapter contains the fullest statement of the thesis, demonstrating the connection among the fact of conscious literary revival, the degree and kind of conscious idealization in the story, and the exposé of the Arthurian legend which paradoxically results from this kind of artistry.

Arthurian Propaganda

1

A Review of
Earlier Malory Scholarship
with Some Suggestions
for Further Studies

The peculiar history of Malory criticism allows one to separate almost all of it into one of three concerns: source study, structural problems, thematic content. Although some of the very recent scholarship covers all three categories, this is only because the earlier work has made a broader view of *Le Morte Darthur* possible. For instance, until it could be shown that the book was something more than a collected translation of continental romances, any responsible investigation of its structure or thematic content would have been considered premature; the existence of an identifiable plan and theme in the book could not be taken for granted. In fact, the direction of Malory criticism has now been brought full circle. The first critical essays were most often written by enthusiasts who waxed lyrical over a work which "arouses all the higher emotions of mankind."[1] Such a book we are repeatedly told has the value of an establishment myth, and it is because of men like its author that "the Eng-

1. C. F. Cooksey, "The Morte d'Arthur," *Nineteenth Century* (June, 1924), pp. 852-59.

[3]

lish aristocracy has long been honoured, nay beloved.''[2] But these essayists were not bothered by the technical problems of authorship, originality and unity; their concern was almost wholly with the nationalistic bias of the book. On the other hand, the majority of early scholars like Malory's editor H. O. Sommer were far more cautious in their approach to the book. Either because of reservations about the insubstantial nature of the book's thematic content, or because of uncertainty about the intention and originality of its supposed author, they confined themselves to rigorous exercises in source study.

This skeptical view of the book reached its height with Vinaver's 1947 edition of the Winchester manuscript. The source studies and structural analyses refuting the views which Vinaver expressed in his Preface and Commentary have for a time precluded any extensive treatment of the book's thematic content, and have necessarily forestalled the possibility of close readings of the text. In general the chief benefit of the books and articles which were written in response to Vinaver's edition[3] is that they have raised Malory's stature as a conscious literary artist and thereby made *Le Morte Darthur* available as a respectable object for literary investigation. Once it is clear that we are dealing with art and not simply translation, it begins to be possible to talk about more than one or two aspects of a work.

It is apparent from the last two years of Malory criticism that a few scholars now feel free to abandon source study in favor of critical interpretations of the book's ideas. Charles Moorman's *The Book of Kyng Arthur* (1965) is a step in this direction. Moorman's primary interest is still with proving the book's unity, but the bulk of his evidence is derived from a thematic analysis. The author acknowledges his debt

2. W. H. Schofield, *Chivalry in English Literature* (Cambridge, 1912), p. 122.

3. See especially J. A. W. Bennett (ed.), *Essays on Malory* (Oxford, 1963); and R. M. Lumiansky (ed.), *Malory's Originality* (Baltimore, 1964).

to the many articles on sources and structure which preceded his study and at the same time claims his independence
from their methods. The most recent book on Malory, by
Edmund Reiss, abandons even the concern for proving the
structural unity of *Le Morte Darthur*. Reiss considers that
the case for unity has been established by Moorman and
others, and so his volume entirely concentrates on how Malory should be read and how the book "functions as a work of
literary art."[4] Both critics demonstrate a new method of
approaching Malory, but neither gives much in the way of
a new interpretation. Although the authors exhibit nothing
of the nationalistic fervor of early commentators on Malory,
they still see the book in the traditional way, as a tragedy
of conflicting loyalties produced by an idealized chivalric
code. What is new is their ability to demonstrate the consistency and complexity of Malory's concern with this problem.

It would be misleading to suppose, however, that the
attacks from those sceptical of Malory's artistry have ceased
altogether as a result of recent articles and books. William
Matthews' recent revolutionary biography of Malory contains
a sly rejoinder to the claims of critics like Moorman and
Reiss: "recent implications that he [Malory] worked with
the glacial celerity of an introspective novelist seem thor-
oughly improbable."[5] Matthews' remark is not at all peevish
or unjustified, since we are well reminded that there are
still vast areas of scholarship pertinent to an understanding
of Malory's themes which have not been explored. Consequently many critical assumptions about Malory's artistry
must seem without adequate rationale to a scholar like Matthews. Many of the scholarly tools and assumptions which
the medievalist relies on quite comfortably in his analysis of
Chaucer's works have not been refined for or applied to *Le
Morte Darthur*. I shall try to indicate the specific problems

4. Edmund Reiss, *Sir Thomas Malory* (New York, 1966), Preface.
5. William Matthews, *The Ill-Framed Knight* (Berkeley, 1966), p.
125.

which need illumination when discussing the three main categories of Malory scholarship, since many of these problems are relevant to the subject of this study.

Several readers have recognized that the political implications of the Arthurian story seem to play a large part in shaping the narrative of Malory's *Le Morte Darthur.* I am concerned with examining this problem in some detail for itself, but primarily for the light it may throw on some other areas of investigation: Malory's conception of tragedy; the hints of apocalyptic thinking which run through the story and are reinforced by the author's individual sense of history; his perception of the interplay of order and chaos in a society which chooses to see life in terms of irreconcilable alternatives; and the exact nature of his appeal to "many noble and dyvers gentylmen of thys royame of Englond."[6] I am not sure that the question of Malory's intention need enter the discussion of all of these aspects of his work. It is not by any means clear that Malory was specifically aware of the ideas I intend to deal with, nor do I see the necessity for proving that he was. What I am trying to understand here are the "givens" of the author's world which would be apparent from the text regardless of his intentions. The background treatises on political theory and social milieu which are indispensable to such a study are discussed in Chapter 2. At this point the Malory scholarship which is either useful or antagonistic to such an investigation is under review.

The division of this criticism into source study, structural concerns, and thematic criticism has some basis in the history of Malory scholarship, as I have indicated. Although in the best criticism these categories overlap, they are treated separately here for the sake of convenience. In dealing with the first of these categories it is necessary to be selective rather than comprehensive in an effort to show the kinds of source

6. Eugene Vinaver (ed.), *The Works of Sir Thomas Malory* (Oxford, 1954), Caxton's Preface, XV. Caxton's literary taste and intentions are a sideline worth investigating.

study that have been done and their relevance to a thematic study of the book even though there is very little source study with any specific bearing on the subject of this discussion.

At the outset it is useful to observe the cautionary advice of two recent critics concerning the limited authority of source study. A comparison of Malory's text with his sources is chancy, as Charles Moorman points out, because we are never sure of having the exact book that Malory worked from; nor can the critic determine the precise proportions with which the author mixed two different sources. And finally it is always possible that ''original'' passages have actually been borrowed from other unknown sources.[7] Further, William Matthews' work on the Armagnac manuscript compiled by Michel Gonnot (Bibliothèque nationale fr. 112) shows methods of organization and compression strikingly similar to those which scholars have always attributed to Malory: ''In large measure it [the Armagnac manuscript of Gonnot] was a procedure of conflating, anthologizing, and arranging; but it also involved some shortening of the excerpts, a good deal of condensation, some concentration on individual heroes, and a fair amount of disentangling and clarifying the narrative *entrelacement* of complicated sections.''[8] Not only are these precisely the methods of composition which Malory used, but Matthews finds more than coincidental evidence actually connecting Malory with the Armagnac manuscripts. For this reason it seems wise to use source study as only a tentative base for generalizations about Malory's thematic designs.

The first extensive source studies were done by Sommer in the third volume of his edition of Malory, and his chief task was simply that of identifying the sources which Malory used. Certainly a significant number of articles since Sommer's day have been content to do the same thing. J. D. Bruce's 1901 article[9] is an early example of this kind of

7. Charles Moorman, *The Book of Kyng Arthur: The Unity of Malory's Morte Darthur* (Lexington, 1965), p. xix.

8. Matthews, *Ill-Framed Knight*, p. 132.

9. J. D. Bruce, ''The Middle-English Metrical Romance 'Le Morte

approach. Bruce works out the source relationship of Malory's last two books, which are generally assumed to be the most original compositions, and when he finds things that do not appear in either the stanzaic poem or the French *Mort Artu* he readily assumes a lost source to account for the discrepancy. He outlines these departures but does not see any thematic or structural pattern in them which would indicate that they are original with Malory.[10] Nevertheless the material he presents has been used for critical interpretation by later scholars.

A somewhat later and more insightful use of sources throws light on the apocalyptic bent of Malory's mind: Laura Hibbard demonstrates that Malory's condensations do not result in a misunderstanding or misrepresentation of a source—as other critics have suggested—but, as in the case of the Balin story, the condensation emphasizes the dramatic qualities of the story which most interest the author.[11] Taking Miss Hibbard's evidence of Malory's narrative skill one step further, we can see that if we are dealing with a conscious innovation here Malory's version purposely makes the Balin story figure forth in small the larger sense of finality which characterizes his interpretation of the entire Arthurian story.

Of the other early source studies Vida Scudder's book *Le Morte Darthur of Sir Thomas Malory and Its Sources* (1921) contains some of the most significant material on the early Arthurian texts. More often than not the book suggests interesting questions about source study which it is not equipped to answer. I have taken some of Miss Scudder's questions and used them as points of departure for the thematic analysis which appears in Chapters 3 and 4. The author is interested in the nature of medieval romance as a vehicle

---

Arthur' (Harleian MS. 2252): Its Sources and Its Relation to Sir Thomas Malory's Morte Darthur,'' *Anglia*, XXIII (1901).

10. *Ibid.*, pp. 67–100.

11. L. A. Hibbard, ''Malory's Book of Balin,'' *Medieval Studies in Memory of G. S. Loomis* (New York, 1927), pp. 175–95.

for self-expression and as an index of medieval life. Whether or not she justifies her opinion that medieval romance is a valid social document, she has proposed a question which is relevant to this study. Miss Scudder sees a direct relation between the coherence of a narrative and the degree of reality which it encompasses; her work on the sources indicates to her that one can see this relationship developing in the changes which Malory made in the narrative structure of his French texts. This premise, however central to our use of source study for thematic ends, is based nevertheless on Miss Scudder's own view of reality; she sees life as "spherical, not linear, coherent, not crumbled, it entangles to resolve, it is centered in crises and advances to climax."[12] Whether we can credit such a view of reality, or even of reality in fiction, to Malory is another question, and some attempt to answer it ought to precede any investigation of the social and political aspects of his work. The degree and kind of causality in romance as it applies to *Le Morte Darthur* ought also to be brought to bear in discussions of this kind. Finally, Miss Scudder notices that Malory's narrative is by turns influenced in the direction of either chronicle or romance depending upon the nature of the source he was using. In Chapter 3 I have identified briefly the specific properties of each genre as a way of understanding their usefulness to Malory and the rationale for and effect of combining them in his peculiar fashion.

It is unfortunate that some of the problems which Miss Scudder turned up did not influence the direction of source investigation in the years following her book, because scholars might have prepared the way for a more sophisticated approach to Malory's themes. Most of the source studies by R. H. Wilson which appeared in the forties are of a more limited kind than Miss Scudder's. Wilson traces source relationships and analogues to incidents in Malory's book, but although he provides some very useful material for the scholar

12. Vida Scudder, *Le Morte Darthur of Sir Thomas Malory and Its Sources* (New York, 1921), p. 183.

who is either looking for original passages or parallels to
particular passages, the source material itself can not always
be trusted for the reasons which Moorman and Matthews
have noted. What is of some interest here, however, is Wilson's work on the names in Malory. His detailed investigations in this area show that while Malory's sources introduce
numerous characters who are left unnamed, Malory reduces
the number of these characters and wherever possible assigns names to the ones he retains. Wilson's numerical evidence suggests that this must have been a conscious technique
on Malory's part and not simply accidental.[13] Whether the
names are borrowed from unknown sources, or whether they
are original with Malory, the facts indicate an interest in
tightening his fictional world by creating a familiar society
of people who recur in successive tales. This material obviously has some bearing on the nature of reality which Malory provides for his book, and perhaps on the social and
political implications which set the book apart from the
vague world depicted in the French sources.

The Commentary in the third volume of Vinaver's edition
of the Winchester manuscript sets passages of Malory's text
against their sources as far as these can be determined. Vinaver's method of source study is his way of assessing Malory's
achievement as a writer. Often Malory is evaluated as if he
were attempting to give the same interpretation and emphasis
to a story as the one he found in his source, and in these instances Vinaver speaks of the writer's "misreadings" and
his narrative "inconsistencies." Naturally the Commentary
is conditioned by the editor's view that the book is a collection
of separate romances, and whatever views one holds on this
subject this theory is bound to lead to what may be a distorted
view of Malory's relation to his source material. In speaking
of the character of Gawain, Vinaver notes the "inconsistencies" of Malory's attitude towards that figure: "Malory does
not attempt to reconcile the two conceptions of Gawain's

13. R. H. Wilson, "Malory's Naming of Minor Characters," *Journal
of English and Germanic Philology*, XLII (1943), 364–85.

character: he blindly accepts the verdict of each of his sources and so produces a picture full of inconsistencies and contradictions."[14] This *a priori* method is obviously a highly conjectural approach to source study, especially when internal evidence, as other scholars have pointed out, shows a high degree of thematic consistency in Malory's development of Gawain.

The reaction to Vinaver's methods of using sources in evaluating Malory constitutes another branch of Malory scholarship and is best represented by the articles in *Malory's Originality*. Since these essays are primarily concerned with sources as a key to structure they will be discussed with the other critical studies of the book's structure. At this point it is only necessary to single out one article on the problem of Gawain which demonstrates that Vinaver's bias has prevented him from making a better use of his vast knowledge of sources. R. M. Lumiansky's article, "Gawain's Miraculous Strength," shows that at least in the matter of strength Malory has made very good thematic use of the two conflicting or "inconsistent" accounts of Gawain's prowess. The "deterioration of relationships" which accelerates the tragedy of the last tale is emphasized by this combination of sources, and not incidentally, the characteristic weakness of Arthur as an example of kingship is underlined.[15] The article is convincing in its analysis of the pertinent source material, and it also allows one to see that Malory was capable of fairly complex characterization (in this case of both Gawain and Arthur). The establishment of these points through the use of sources is an essential step towards any discussion of Malory's conception of history and tragedy.

Vinaver's recent revised edition of Malory's works admits few modifications of his views. Indeed it is unlikely that his approach to source study will ever allow itself to uncover

14. Eugene Vinaver (ed.), *The Works of Sir Thomas Malory* (Oxford, 1947), III, 1423.
15. R. M. Lumiansky, "Gawain's Miraculous Strength: Malory's Use of *Le Morte Arthur* and *Mort Artu*," *Etudes Anglaises*, X (1957), 97–108.

material which will aid a study of Malory's ideas, because it is predisposed to treat Malory as if he had no ideas. It is strange, then, that although Vinaver's treatment of *Le Morte Darthur* is naive, his comments on the French romances should be so sophisticated. In this area his edition is more valuable than almost anything else in the field of source study. Vinaver has raised and answered many of the questions about the structure and materials of the Vulgate cycle that Miss Scudder had proposed in reference to Malory. His contribution here is not so much in ascribing specific sources for passages in Malory's text as it is in filling out the cultural context of the French material. Unfortunately these ideas have not been fully used as a way of defining the milieu of Malory's book which sets it apart from that of its sources.

It is obvious from this outline of the kinds of source study which have been done on *Le Morte Darthur* that the book could still benefit from much more clarification of its backgrounds. Further studies ought to include some exploration of Malory's sense of distance (either historical or ideological, or both) from both his French and English sources; a clearer and more useful definition of what the meanings of *translator* were for the fifteenth century, and some indication of the relevance of this definition to Malory's work; and a closer look at the interplay of romance and chronicle in the book based on a more precise understanding of what constituted each genre for the medieval writer than has been employed to date. D. S. Brewer in his essay " 'The hoole book' " (1963), has written briefly on this matter, noting that Malory has handled his sources in such a way as to increase the historical nature of the story.[16] This is an interesting idea, but a good deal more needs to be done to make it useful and convincing. Finally, the principles or rules of source study as they apply to Malory's work ought to be more firmly established: we want to know what the limits of a conjectural approach are, and how to establish the relative importance of innovation to

16. D. S. Brewer, " 'The hoole book,' " *Essays on Malory*, ed. J. A. W. Bennett (Oxford, 1963), p. 49.

straight borrowing. All of these questions about source study are pertinent to thematic investigations, and without some clarification of these points the directions which thematic studies can take are limited.

The nature of the scholarship on the structure of *Le Morte Darthur* took an abrupt turn in 1947 when Vinaver published his edition of the Winchester manuscript and announced that *Le Morte Darthur* as a single work had ceased to exist. *The Works of Sir Thomas Malory*, its successor, presents eight self-contained romances dealing with the same Arthurian material representing successive stages in the development of Malory's prose style. But according to Vinaver's reading of the explicits between the tales in the Winchester manuscript these romances do not form a continuous narrative. Unfortunately one suspects in reading Vinaver's Preface and Commentary that he has arrived at this theory because he never really believed Malory was as competent a craftsman as the authors of his French sources. Several hostile replies to his edition have suggested as much. But regardless of his motives Vinaver's edition has stimulated more interest in Malory than any other scholarship on the subject before or since its publication. The reason for this interest is not simply a result of vested interests in the continuous narrative theory, although that has been part of it; but also Vinaver has revealed that there are some very important questions to be asked about the nature of narrative structure in *Le Morte Darthur*.

It is not necessary or even possible to summarize in detail the arguments for and against Vinaver's theory of separate romances, since the articles in *Malory's Originality* perform this function in their defense of the book's unity. Because so few articles have emerged in Vinaver's defense, recent critics have underscored their conviction that the case for unity has been won. There is of course the possibility that there are partisans of Vinaver who have not defended him in print because he has been able to do such an energetic job on his own behalf. Out of all this controversy only one thing is certain—the debate about separate romances has become boring in addition to being barren. Fruitful and consistent readings of *Le Morte Darthur* will retain their value even if their assumptions about the book's unity (or lack of it) prove incorrect. Any piece of criticism that would lose its value if the separate romance theory were conclusively proven would have to have been flabby to begin with. What is of greater interest now are those still unsolved problems encountered by recent critics in their examination of the book's structure. Most of these problems have a definite relationship to the kind of thematic work which can be done on Malory's book in the future. As with the matter of source study, there are several gaps in our knowledge which limit the scope of future investigations of the book's themes.

There are still important technical problems to be explored in the book's structure. The question of whether *Le Morte Darthur* possesses historical unity (intended by the author), or critical unity (unity which exists regardless of intention), or both, or neither, has usually been decided in favor of the view that it possesses both kinds of unity.[17] There may be more sides to this question, however, now that the main part of the argument is decided, or there may be more ways of exploring the peculiar kind of unity which we confront in Malory's book. The first possible approach to this problem is through the investigation of fictional time in the book, which I will deal with in Chapters Two and Three. A second approach may lie in establishing a more flexible definition of plot, appropriate to Malory's book though not to the modern novel. D. S. Brewer has done the most sensible work on this problem to date, because his definition of the kind of plot Malory uses also instructs the modern reader in how to read the book. He does not attempt to uncover a unified plot as we know it, but sees instead "a continuous stream of development (as in, say, a biography), with well marked

17. Moorman, *The Book of Kyng Arthur,* p. xvii.

pauses. But the pauses are all stations on the same journey; not termini of different lines.''[18]

Rumble and Moorman have discerned another pattern to describe Malory's plot structure; it involves what Rumble calls ''development by analogy.''[19] The system of contrasting or parallel situations in the book is not simply a result of the similarities found between separate events in Malory's sources; these parallels as Malory uses them are very closely tied to the demands of his theme. In short, the work of these two critics and those who have cooperated with them, implies a large degree of causality in the composition of Malory's plot or plots. What I have tried to include in my discussion of the book's themes is an investigation of the degree and kind of causality in Malory's book as compared with the narrative techniques of the sources. But this kind of work must also be done in the light of the Armagnac manuscript which Matthews describes as similar to Malory in techniques of compression and emphasis. Such a study would be useful to critics interested in the nature of tragedy as Malory sees it. It is hard to conceive of tragedy without causality and without sequential time, and yet both elements have been denied Malory by critics who nevertheless affirm that a conflict of two goods produces a powerful sense of tragedy at the end of the book.

The nature of tragedy and sequential time also involves a study of the kind of fictional time found in *Le Morte Darthur*. It is now generally recognized that the eccentric time scheme of the book is a consequence of what Lumiansky has called ''retrospective narrative.''[20] Malory's reliance on this internal time scheme has been worked out in great detail by Moorman and T. L. Wright, so that the literal sequence of events

18. D. S. Brewer, ''Form in the *Morte Darthur*,'' *Medium Aevum*, XXI (1952), 16.

19. Thomas C. Rumble, '' 'The Tale of Tristram': Development by Analogy,'' *Malory's Originality*, ed. R. M. Lumiansky (Baltimore, 1964), pp. 118–83.

20. R. M. Lumiansky, ''The Question of Unity in Malory's *Morte Darthur*,'' *Tulane Studies in English*, V (1955), 38.

in the book is no longer a serious obstacle to readers who are willing to recognize that Malory sees time in terms of theme.[21] Very recently Edmund Reiss has noticed another kind of thematic pattern in Malory's references to time. Most of these latter indications of time are appropriately attached to an important holy day in the Church calendar, and taken together "all the actions in the long narrative are symbolically pushed together to occupy, as it were, one moment in time, one week in the Christian year.''[22] If Reiss's idea were worked out in greater detail it might be possible to see a symbolic structure in Malory's chronology. As it is, I have found that Reiss's suggestions fit very well with a theory of kingship based on the political theology which Ernst Kantorowicz describes.[23] If Malory sees the events of Arthur's reign as a kind of temporal parallel to the spiritual events which mark off time in the history of the Church, we then have a new direction for critical interpretations of the book. But before one could undertake a study of this sort it would be essential to know something about the conventions of representing time in medieval fiction and the kind of apocalyptic thinking which may have surrounded medieval interpretations of the Arthurian story. It may be that Malory himself will turn out to be the only reliable source of information on the laws of fictional time in his narrative, but even if this is true someone will still need to study exactly how these laws operate in *Le Morte Darthur*.

The mechanics of editing medieval manuscripts constitutes another area of investigation which has far reaching implications for our interpretation of the literature and our perception of its structure. It is odd that with all the arguments

21. Charles Moorman, ''Internal Chronology in Malory's *Morte Darthur*,'' *Journal of English and Germanic Philology*, LX (1961), 240–49. T. L. Wright, '' 'The Tale of King Arthur': Beginnings and Foreshadowings,'' *Malory's Originality*, ed. R. M. Lumiansky (Baltimore, 1964), pp. 9–66.

22. Reiss, *Sir Thomas Malory*, p. 39.

23. Ernst Kantorowicz, *The King's Two Bodies: A Study of Medieval Political Theology* (Princeton, 1957).

over the book's unity, the preliminary work defining what the term *book* meant to a fifteenth-century reader has never been examined in detail as it applies to the problems of structure in *Le Morte Darthur*. On the most basic level, R. H. Wilson has tried to define what the word *tale* meant to Malory as a way of interpreting the function of the explicits between the eight major divisions of the book. The divisions between tales occur at points where Malory changes his source, so *tale* may simply be defined as a body of narrative drawn from a particular source; or Malory may use the word *tale* to refer to subdivisions within the eight major sections (e.g., the Balin story or the Wedding of Arthur).[24] In either case we have no clear evidence that Malory thought of these sections as separate compositions. Thomas Rumble has also indicated that the finality of Vinaver's divisions of the narrative results from Vinaver's individual paragraphing of the first explicit. As Rumble reads the manuscript the phrase "this book endyth" may well refer only to Malory's source.[25] Matthews mentions in passing the three possible meanings of *book* for the fifteenth century: "a division within a single work; a complete work with a single set of covers; a series of separately bound volumes on the same subject."[26] Regardless of the establishment of the book's unity, no one has gone into the matter of how the fifteenth-century reader or writer would have defined the word *book*, and how he would thus have looked at Malory's manuscript.

Two somewhat related points which need investigation follow from the suggestions outlined above. First there is a question of that perspective in *Le Morte Darthur* which we are not used to encountering in modern works. Tournaments and battles are described at greater length and in more detail than the great crises of human events in the book: we see far less of Arthur than we do of Palomydes; the love

24. R. H. Wilson, "How Many Books Did Malory Write?" *University of Texas Studies in English*, XXX (1951), 5.

25. Thomas C. Rumble, "The First *Explicit* in Malory's *Morte Darthur*," *Modern Language Notes*, LXXI (1956), 564–66.

26. Matthews, *Ill-Framed Knight*, p. 79.

affair of Lancelot and Guinevere occupies considerably less narrative space than Tristram's jousts. Early critics unsympathetic to Malory criticized him for lacking a sense of fitness and proportion, but obviously something can be learned about his narrative method and his way of seeing the world from his disproportionate emphasis on the "trivia" of daily life in Arthurian society. In my discussion of Tale V and elsewhere I have offered explanations of Malory's narrative perspective. Also, critics are not accustomed to speak of Malory as though he had a narrative voice. Brief passages of overt moralizing are cited as the translator's imposition of his point of view on the material he borrows. Other passages which serve a similar function are less easy to recognize because they are often speeches written in for characters like Arthur in Tale II, Dinadan in the Tristram section, and the hermit in the Fair Maid of Astolat section of Tale VII. Throughout Chapters Three and Four I have followed up these "intrusions" to discover what kind of commentary they form on the context in which they appear, and—taken together—whether they form a coherent point of view.

In contrast to the large amount of work done on the sources and structure of *Le Morte Darthur* scholars have been reluctant to explore its thematic content. The reasons for their reluctance are not difficult to determine. Many critics have been waiting for source study to establish the book as a respectable work—important, original, and full of those ideas which the critic feels adequate to deal with. Now we can see that no amount of source study will be able to satisfy the critic on these points. I have already suggested that some of the structural aspects of the book do not immediately captivate the modern reader because he is bound to feel that there is a kind of sloppiness and a large measure of the accidental in its composition, and that therefore it does not graciously lend itself to dissection by his critical tools. Furthermore, the thematic importance of the book has never been established except on the "lower cultural level"; it is not in the canon of books which scholars discuss for intellectual content. The questionable matter of the degree of originality in the book also robs the critic of any certainty about the artist's conscious intention, and his critical methods often do not operate without that certainty. But all of these objections are hardly valid commentaries on the merits of the book. There is indeed a question about how closely we are justified in reading Malory's text; but if a close reading of the book is inappropriate, other approaches to it are not therefore also invalid. The suggestions made above for future work on sources and structure are all intended to help the critic understand *how* to read the book and what kinds of investigations are most likely to yield interesting results. To discuss as many critics wish to, what Malory thought about chivalry, courtly love, and Christianity may not be the most rewarding avenue of criticism, because his views of these three institutions are very likely of secondary importance in his narrative. It might be more useful to begin instead by considering what we can understand of the book's political context, the view of time which it displays, the nature of reality in its narrative, and the conception of tragedy operating in the last tales, and to leave the problem of the three institutions in abeyance.

A brief summary of what critics have thought the book was ''about'' reveals a striking similarity in their approach and opinion. Two aspects of the book have been at the center of most of these thematic studies: the first is Malory's treatment of chivalry, and the second is the conflict of loyalties to God, King, and Lady which produce the final tragedy. It has become axiomatic to speak of Malory's great reverence for the aristocratic virtues of chivalry. Even though many critics recognize that the final catastrophe is some indication that the worldly fellowship is inadequate, they nevertheless imply that its failure is built into the plot and that the author himself never loses faith in the ''unfailing merits of Arthurian chivalry . . . and the undisputed greatness of its protagonist.''[27] Considerable disagreement exists as to wheth-

27. P. E. Tucker, ''The Place of the 'Quest of the Holy Grail' in the 'Morte Darthur,' '' *Modern Language Review*, XLVIII (1953), 392.

er Malory's chivalry is highly idealistic or essentially practical, but few critics deny that Malory sees chivalry as anything but an essential good. Even Arthur Ferguson, aware of the marginal status of chivalry in Malory's day, maintains that the "unifying principle in Malory's total work is the social meaning and intellectual consistency of chivalric ideals."[28]

This view of Malory certainly fits with Caxton's Preface to his edition, but Caxton had peculiar tastes and interests of his own which may have led him to establish this moral reading of Malory to suit his pocketbook and his social status. The manuscripts which Caxton published throughout his career demonstrate that his taste was antiquarian and that his intentions were simply those of an aficionado with a wealthy audience to please. We therefore need to reconsider the wisdom of reading Malory in the light of Caxton's Preface, especially since Caxton was anxious to prove to his aristocratic patrons that Malory upheld the seedy virtues of chivalry which they presumably cherished. We have also a strong hint in the Preface that he did not feel quite comfortable with Malory's book, that he felt the need to apologize for, or dismiss politely, those parts of it which did not square with his "moral interpretation." All of this points to the flaw in our assuming that Caxton's proximity in time to the composition of the book makes him the best authority on its themes. "Many noble and dyvers gentylmen of thys royame of Englond" may have gleaned from *Le Morte Darthur* a comforting moral message reinforcing their love of chivalric pastimes which is not there. So far no one has attempted to distinguish the thematic interpretation which Caxton placed on Malory's book both in his Preface and in his methods of editing the manuscript for print from the themes in the book as Malory left it. Vinaver does make a distinction between what he sees as Caxton's moral concern

28. Arthur B. Ferguson, *The Indian Summer of English Chivalry: Studies in the Decline and Transformation of Chivalric Idealism* (Durham, N.C., 1960), p. 46.

with chivalry and the totally practical chivalry which he finds in Malory, but he assumes an equal reverence for the institution on the part of both men with the difference that Malory was less sophisticated about its moral implications.

Both Caxton and Vinaver give us a very simple Malory; between them they have reduced his thematic content to almost nothing. Both editors either by implication or by direct accusation find that Malory indulges himself in a nostalgia for a world long dead—this is an obvious corollary to the traditional view of Malory's worship of chivalry. One would expect that early essayists like those quoted in the beginning of this chapter would have seen Malory as a nostalgic writer; but surprisingly we find that many recent critics also read the book as a manifestation of a "desire to oversimplify or to turn away from the present."[29] A few critics on the other side of this issue see *Le Morte Darthur* as politically inspired—an allegory of the times. Unfortunately those readers have attempted to draw parallels between Arthur and his knights and the great personages of Malory's day; but most of their conjectures are based upon the early biographical material which is now invalid. Although critics disagree about Malory's point of view here, they all speak of the intensely patriotic spirit of the book as though it had been composed as a kind of national epic; and yet none of them has explored the nature of this "nationalism" and whether it has political implications in the book.

The weakness of approaching Malory's themes in the ways outlined above is that once one has established Malory's interest in chivalric virtues, whether nostalgic or not, and once the meaning of the book's action is described in terms of conflicting loyalties, the book is virtually "explained away." Its content has been simplified out of existence and we are likely to get the impression that there is little else to talk about in the book. Fortunately a paradox is inherent in maintaining that both of these themes are the substance of Malory's interpretation of the Arthurian story.

29. Reiss, *Sir Thomas Malory*, pp. 19–20.

One recent critic has become dissatisfied with the traditional reading of the story as a tragedy produced by the conflicting loyalties which inhere in the chivalric code. In his article "Malory's Tragic Knights" Charles Moorman abandons the view of the book put forth in *The Book of Kyng Arthur* and at last exposes the paradoxes of reading the book in the traditional way. He asks why if Malory intended to praise chivalry did he conclude his book by condemning it.[30] There is, he admits, a didactic strain in Malory's treatment of chivalry, but the inevitable failure of the code tends to undermine the didacticism so that "where artistry and the desire for reform conflict . . . it is clear that Malory prefers a consistent tragic book to an ill-formed moral one."[31] Moorman no longer sees the ending as the tragedy of two conflicting goods; he finds that this conflict between artistry and reform produces a tone of total despair at the end which is not redeemed by any "upsurge of spirit" or "illumination of self."[32] This article is the first real hint that the issues in the book are significantly different from those traditionally offered and vastly more complex than readers have acknowledged to date.

Moorman has really presented only a dilemma in the interpretation of Malory, since within the scope of his article he was able to do little more than outline his position. As I see it, the center of the problem he exposed is that *Le Morte Darthur* has always been read as the straightforward conflict of two goods, and the reader has been forced, therefore, to distort and simplify the themes of the book to fit the rather facile tragic ending which the critic has framed for it. Although Moorman's revised interpretation of the book may not be acceptable, he has demonstrated the necessity of redefining the kind of tragedy which actually exists in the book by uncovering the real issues which Malory treated.

30. Charles Moorman, "Malory's Tragic Knights," *Mediaeval Studies* (Toronto), XXVII (1965), 120.
31. *Ibid.*, p. 119.
32. *Ibid.*, p. 124.

2

Medieval Political Theory and the Arthurian Legend

The foregoing analysis of Malory scholarship demonstrates that the kinds of work done on Chaucer's cultural and intellectual milieu—so helpful to the Chaucer critic—do not exist for Malory. Critics have ignored the importance of this background material in studying Malory because they have too often assumed that *Le Morte Darthur* was simply one more addition to the unbroken line of Arthurian narratives. They have therefore not recognized that with Malory we confront a purposeful and conscious revival of Arthurian material which arises out of a cultural context very different from that of Geoffrey, the earlier English Arthurian poems, or the French Vulgate Cycle—a context specifically related to the contemporary aristocratic concern with reliving the ceremonies and traditions of the past. In this chapter I will outline a background in medieval English historiography and political theory to be used here and later to indicate a number of things about the themes of *Le Morte Darthur* and its place in the development of the Arthurian story.

Besides the inclusion of these specifically medieval background materials, I intend here and later to employ certain
theories of social organization to account for the nature of
the story and the individual turn which it received at Malory's hands. This material on social theory is not simply
grafted onto a literary interpretation of *Le Morte Darthur*
but grows out of a close comparison of the book with its
sources and out of a study of the book in its cultural milieu.

Whatever may be said by those critics who find Malory
less "authentic," less complex, and more mundane than his
French predecessors, the lasting appeal of the story as we
have it now is largely attributable to his version. Part of
the nature of Malory's retelling is that it lays bare what is
tragic and endlessly captivating about the Arthurian story.
Sometimes inadvertently, and sometimes by design, he has
exposed certain basic elements of the story which had remained carefully concealed in the versions of his predecessors.
His vantage point in time peculiarly suited him for a retelling
which would by refashioning the story, expose some of its
nerves. Strangely enough Malory's misunderstandings and
"mishandling" of the subtleties of his sources tell us as
much about the true nature of Arthurian legend as any
amount of research into the origins of the myth. What Denis
de Rougemont said about the sources of a myth in his analysis of the Tristan story holds true for the entire Arthurian
story as well: "A myth arises whenever it becomes dangerous
or impossible to speak plainly about certain social or religious matters, or affective relations, and yet there is a
desire to preserve these or else it is impossible to destroy
them."[1] In the case of the Tristan story, de Rougemont uncovers the fact that the myth is used to express "the dark and
unmentionable fact that passion is linked with death."[2] The
true nature of the social matters which lurk beneath the surface of the Arthurian story can be exposed in a similar

1. Denis de Rougemont, *Love in the Western World* (New York,
1940), p. 21.
2. *Ibid.*

fashion when the myth is "mishandled" by a man who takes it as a valid ideal of life, employs it initially as a realistic guide for his age, and then turns this idealization back on itself, exposing the very fundamental weaknesses of the Arthurian structure. There can be little doubt that those ideas or truths which the Arthurian myth was originally intended to conceal are, as in the case of the Tristan story, the very reason for the story's lasting popularity. Malory's version of the story is particularly interesting, then, because his innovations in the structure of the story and his new thematic design allow us to see what the previously undefined appeal of these hidden truths is.

It is apparent from the scholarship discussed in Chapter 1 that Malory has always been seen as reasonably satisfied with the glories of Arthurian society. Where doubt has been cast on this assumption it has always been directed toward the last two books, and the most any critic has ventured to say was that Malory sharpened the tragic effect of the conflicting loyalties to God, king and lady which inhere in the chivalric code while at the same time never losing confidence in the basic virtues of chivalry. The most succinct and complete statement of this interpretation occurs in an article by Charles Moorman.[3] Moorman traces the book's structure in terms of Aristotelian tragedy: there are three distinct movements representing the rise, flowering, and decay of Arthurian knighthood. Furthermore, according to Moorman, the downfall of the nearly perfect society results first from the three conflicting loyalties, and secondly from the Round Table's inability to live up to the code which Malory inserts in Tale I. At each feast of the Pentecost, Malory says, the knights were sworn, "never to do outerage nothir morthir, and allwayes to fle treson, and to gyff mercy unto him that askith mercy, uppon payne of forfiture [of their] worship and lordship of kynge Arthure for evirmore; and allwayes to do

3. Charles Moorman, "'Lot and Pellinore: The Failure of Loyalty in Malory's 'Morte Darthur,'" *Mediaeval Studies* (Toronto) XXV (1963), 83–92.

ladyes, damesels, and jantilwomen and wydowes [socour]: strengthe hem in hir ryghtes, and never to enforce them, uppon payne of dethe. Also, that no man take no batayles in a wrongefull quarell for no love ne for no worldis goodis" (91).[4] That this code itself may be inadequate to fulfill the needs of governing a country does not occur to Moorman.

Taking this article as the orthodox view of the book's meaning, one may see that in his subsequent article, "Malory's Tragic Knights," and in the essay on Malory in *A Knyght There Was*, Moorman has taken a second look at the nature of the book's tragedy and has changed his mind about its meaning.[5] He recognizes a peculiar tension between the didacticism of Malory's faith in chivalry as a world-saving ideal for his contemporaries and the fact that the book also damns chivalry in no uncertain terms. Moorman's work leads one to suppose that this thematic tension is a product of Malory's own uncertainty about his material and that it is therefore left unresolved. It follows from this view of the book that Moorman must see the last tale in an existential light: the tragedy occurs without any illumination on the part of the tragic figures. They simply fall in ignorance of the real circumstances which led to their defeat. Again Moorman is unclear about the emptiness which he describes. Does it result from the author's inability to reconcile his didacticism with his artistic sense of tragedy, and does Malory also remain ignorant of the story's meaning? Unlike other critics, Moorman does realize that Malory's portrayal of chivalry is profoundly negative in the end, even tragic. Yet we still do not know what the sources of this portrayal are—whether they stem from the author's misunderstanding of the limited perfection required of earthly chivalry, or whether chivalry is responsibly and accurately condemmed on its own terms.

I have discussed Moorman's work at length because it is

4. This and all subsequent page references to *Le Morte Darthur* refer to Eugene Vinaver (ed.), *The Works of Sir Thomas Malory* (Oxford, 1954).

5. Charles Moorman, *A Knyght There Was: The Evolution of the Knight in Literature* (Lexington, 1967), pp. 96ff.

the first piece of scholarship to date to recognize the complexity of the issues involved in *Le Morte Darthur.* But
Moorman has necessarily oversimplified the problem by attributing the tension which he has uncovered in the book to
Malory's own confusion about his intention or his naïve despair about the nature of chivalry. The scope of his article
does not allow him to show how Malory condemns chivalry,
nor does he have room to answer his own question concerning Malory's reasons for doing so. The examination here of
the nature and function of Arthurian chivalry as an historical
ideal of life with political implications is intended to supply
an answer to this question and to exonerate Malory from the
charges of confusion and uncertainty. Moorman has gone
so far as to explain that "the failure of the knights lies not
so much in their code as in their failure . . . to examine themselves and the institutions by which they live."[6] He has not
seen that these failures are reciprocal, that the individual
has been predisposed to fail by the inadequacy of his code.
Some knowledge of the structure of social organizations will
be useful in clarifying this cause and effect relation of the
Round Table's demise.

As we have seen in Chapter 1 a certain amount of critical
attention has always been directed toward possible political
interpretations of Malory's book. The biographical basis for
much of this work has inhibited its success. To read *Le Morte
Darthur* as a political allegory of contemporary conditions is
to miss the really significant issues of the book. Similarly,
to regard the book as an establishment myth intended to
reinforce values already existing in the ruling class of the
time is to distort the book's themes. For this reason the more
sophisticated critics have in recent years ignored the book's
political implications altogether. There is, however, one
recent article by A. L. Morton which suggests a more profit-
able approach to this problem.[7] Morton implies that there

6. *Ibid.,* p. 125.
7. A. L. Morton, "The Matter of Britain," *Zeitschrift für Anglistik
und Amerikanistik,* VIII, no. 1 (1960), 5–28.

may be a connection between the ideal of chivalry and the
political theory which lies behind Malory's reading of the
Arthurian legend. The aristocracy of any age seems predisposed to attach itself to a highly idealistic and often totally
impractical system. As Arthur Ferguson has shown in *The
Indian Summer of English Chivalry*, by the fifteenth century
chivalry had shed most of its practical aspects, while at the
same time the aristocracy insisted upon reviving its rituals
and acting as though knighthood retained the same functions
that it had had in the twelfth and thirteenth centuries.[8]
Morton sees Malory as the spokesman for the ideals of this
class who attempted to give their idea of chivalry some basis
in political reality. He analyzes Malory's intention and his
failure in political terms:

One of the great themes of medieval literature is the perpetual
conflict between the interest of the feudal ruling class *as a whole*
and the interest of the feudal lord as an individual, resulting in a
complex interplay of loyalty and treason, honour and faith breaking, which has no conclusion and, in the end, was one of the reasons
for the decay of feudal society. The Round Table was an attempt
on the ideal plane . . . to resolve this contradiction, but it remained
ideal, because the material basis on which Arthur's company rested
is always left undefined.[9]

Morton's analysis of Malory's conception of the Round
Table's function is especially impressive because he has
reached this conclusion without drawing on fifteenth-century
materials dealing with kingship and social structure. We
shall see that there were indeed specific issues of great interest to political minds of the fifteenth century which reappear in Malory's book. Although they are more varied
and complex than Morton's thesis suggests, they do relate
to the place of kingship in society in the way that he has
outlined here. A knowledge of this material and a close

8. Arthur Ferguson, *The Indian Summer of English Chivalry: Studies in the Decline and Transformation of Chivalric Idealism* (Durham,
N. C., 1960).
9. Morton, ''The Matter of Britain,'' p. 13.

reading of *Le Morte Darthur* do not lead one to Morton's conclusion that Arthurian society failed because it lacked a substantial material basis. In Malory's book this problem is only one aspect of a larger question which lies at the center of the tragedy as he sees it.

The two articles by Moorman and Morton represent the two major aspects of the problem at hand: the nature of the chivalric ideal which Malory was proposing and the political implications of his book. It is in the interaction of these two problems that we find the thematic center of *Le Morte Darthur*. That is, Malory began by recreating in literary form the historical ideal of life which his aristocratic contemporaries cherished, namely that of Arthurian chivalry; and there is a good amount of evidence in his book that this literary recreation was intended initially as a valid political model to be imitated in actual life. As Morton suggests, Malory regarded the Round Table as the ideal solution to the political and moral conflicts which threaten society. But Malory discovered that the very idealism of this structure was designed not to alleviate but to disguise and repress these conflicts in such a way that it eventually annihilated its own powers to coerce its members. Malory's attempt to use the Arthurian legend as an historical ideal of life leads him to uncover the fact that Arthurian society actually provided itself with a means by which all of the conflicts which were eventually to destroy it could continue to operate unacknowledged by the members of the society.

Before turning to the political bias which informs Malory's reading of the story, we need to establish the fact that for the Middle Ages and especially for the later English Middle Ages, the Arthurian story claimed the status of history. Laura Keeler's study of the chroniclers who followed Geoffrey of Monmouth demonstrates their remarkable tendency to take Geoffrey's account of Arthur as the record of an actual historical figure. Some chroniclers, of course, add the material about the Round Table and exaggerate Arthur's military accomplishments, while others question the veracity of Geoffrey's treatment of the story: but there is almost no material which suggests that Arthur and his knights are fictitious figures.[10] As Johan Huizinga has pointed out, the sense of history in an age "springs up wherever a phase of culture has its spiritual center."[11] In the Middle Ages history was not an academic discipline; the medieval sense of the past was grounded instead in certain ideals of its past. Legend, chronicle, and myth were repositories of history for the Middle Ages; these forms contained "images of its past."[12] The evidence of the chroniclers after Geoffrey—as well as Huizinga's statements on medieval historiography—ought therefore to impress upon us the fact that Malory must have taken the Arthurian story seriously as the description of an actual society.

But if Arthurian society was an actual epoch in English history for Malory, it was certainly far more than that. It had for Malory as for many of his contemporaries the value of what Huizinga calls an "historical ideal of life." Huizinga defines such ideals not in terms of their precise historical reality but in terms of their value for the age which chooses to recreate them: "The historical accuracy of a concept is for the moment of no importance; the only thing that matters is whether it appeared to its advocates to be the true picture of a past reality. . . . Hence a historical life-ideal may be defined as any concept of excellence man projects into the past."[13] It is essential to an understanding of Malory to recognize that historical ideals, however remote from reality, are intended to fulfill actual needs for the society which revives them. In the analysis of *Le Morte Darthur* we see that the function which the historical ideal of Arthurian chivalry was to serve was a quasi-political one. In his analysis of chivalry as an historical ideal Huizinga shows

10. Laura Keeler, "Geoffrey of Monmouth and the Late Latin Chroniclers," *University of California Publications in English*, XVII, no. 1 (1946).
11. Johan Huizinga, *Men and Ideas* (New York, 1959), p. 38.
12. *Ibid.*, p. 41.
13. *Ibid.*, p. 80.

that chivalry in the later Middle Ages was valued, among other things, as the active expression of what we might call a political theory: "they required a form for their political thought, and here the idea of chivalry came in. Thanks to the chivalric fiction history was reduced . . . to a noble game with edifying and heroic rules."[14]

By taking the historical ideal of his contemporaries and identifying it with Arthurian chivalry in particular, Malory also attempted to make this ideal of life serve a political end. The important thing to recognize, however, is that Malory assigned a definite cultural function to Arthurian chivalry, and the political idealism of the book is simply an extension of this cultural function. Because he could only understand his picture of the past as it functioned in the present, in his own culture, he tried either consciously or unconsciously, to make the Arthurian story correspond to the political theory of his day. Perhaps it would be more accurate to say that he read the Arthurian romances as though they illustrated the virtues which fifteenth-century political theory held most important. In any case, what we discover from examining the structure, sources, and themes of *Le Morte Darthur* is a surprising emphasis upon issues closely related to those of fifteenth-century political theology and, more particularly, to the theory or fiction of the King's Two Bodies. Ernst Kantorowicz has studied this matter in great detail.[15] The precise issues of this theory will be considered in some detail later, but for the moment it will suffice to outline its political and cultural purpose. The whole fiction of the King's Two Bodies seems to be a legalistic and highly artificial way of assuring the continuity of political forms throughout time despite the deaths of kings, the dissolution of parliaments, and the accidents of civil war. This theory also provides a way of justifying faith and confidence in the value of human institutions, because it is primarily concerned with perpet-

14. *Ibid.*, p. 199.
15. Ernst Kantorowicz, *The King's Two Bodies: A Study in Mediaeval Political Theology* (Princeton, 1957).

uating those institutions. Obviously these were crucial matters in the troubled fifteenth century, so that it is not surprising to find that they received their fullest statement in
the writings of Sir John Fortescue at the time of the Wars
of the Roses.

For Malory, chivalry was to be the practical means for
instituting and maintaining the governmental structure
which fifteenth-century political theory called for. Arthurian society seems to have attracted Malory's attention because
he thought it corresponded to the corporational thinking of
his time and that it was therefore perfectly designed to
demonstrate the way in which governmental structures are
secured and perpetuated. There is no reason to try to prove
that Malory was capable of or interested in working out the
intricate legal theory which accompanied the political writing
of his time. Nevertheless, the thematic analyses in Chapters
3 and 4 do show that he was aware of the major political
issues of his day and that these found their way into his
retelling of the Arthurian story. What emerges from this
explanation of the function that Arthurian chivalry was
chosen to serve in *Le Morte Darthur* is an understanding of
the thematic tension which Moorman has recognized but not
explained. The demands which Malory's political thinking
made on the story could not be satisfied. The tenets of the
theory of the King's Two Bodies, with its insistence on the
continuity of government, exposed the inadequacies of chivalry and especially Arthurian chivalry as political institutions.
The incompatibility between the themes of the Arthurian
story and the political idealism which Malory introduces as
a standard for judging the Arthurian structure produces the
tension which makes his version of the tragedy unique.

It is hard to say with any degree of assurance that Malory
began his translations knowing that the Arthurian story was
a poor vehicle for the political *sen* of his book and that he
therefore must have intended *Le Morte Darthur* as an object
lesson on government for his own times. But it is far more
tenuous to suppose that as he proceeded with his scheme of

presenting the Arthurian legend as a pure cultural ideal, the material simply became less tractable with respect to his own political views, leading him to expose the weaknesses of the society he had intended to praise. What I am arguing for is simply the recognition that Malory's presentation of the story is a highly complex one: he creates for the story of Arthur the aura of an historical ideal and at the same time robs it of that prestige. We can only assume that he both intended and understood the failure of Arthurian chivalry to constitute a viable political model. Certainly the original material of the last three tales argues strongly for Malory's having had such a conscious plan throughout *Le Morte Darthur.*

Both the political theory and the cultural values of his time were dedicated not to the ideal of progress, but to the establishment of world peace.[16] It seems quite natural, then, that to Malory's contemporaries chivalry should have appeared well suited for the attainment of this goal. The strong degree of altruism and asceticism inherent in the Arthurian code are ostensibly dedicated to the abandonment of individual goals for the stabilization of the community. As the narrative progresses, however, we find that these "virtues" of Arthurian society can not be pressed into the service of world peace without changing the whole direction of the story. Rather than do that, Malory seems to have chosen to exploit the tragic possibilities inhering in the illusory nature of the "ideal" civilization. The political theory of his own time gave him the leverage with which he exposed the illusions of the past.

The problem of exactly what happens to Arthur in Malory's hands is difficult because it is double edged. The final exposé of the Round Table society as an inadequate vessel of human glory and achievement has, of course, the inevitable Christian dimension. That is, the ideal passes away because everything on earth passes away; the promise of perfection is a promise unfulfilled even in the lives of kings. This is the

16. Huizinga, *Men and Ideas*, p. 82.

emotional and spiritual message which one gets from every version of the Arthurian story no matter how truncated or cheapened or modernized. Malory reinforces this aspect of the tragic effect by cutting us off from the possibility of further idealization of Arthur and from the hope of new life from old sources. The cumulative effect of Malory's tragedy is that of separation from the past and from the notion of recreating the past. For his time especially this was an unexpected conclusion. Arthurian materials had long been a testament not only to what might have been but *also* to what men still hoped might be. People coveted the notion of Arthur's return, courts seriously imitated the Round Table, and the aristocracy saw the salvation of the country in the rituals of chivalric perfection as they were embodied in Arthur's reign. The final tragedy of Malory's *Morte* is its picture of Arthur desolate and cut off; this vignette speaks also for Malory's times, because his rendering of the story has cut his contemporaries off from the most precious of their illusions about the redemptive force and promise of their past.

By now there should be no question of treating Malory's book as quaint or nostalgic. There is a great difference between the rather childish Arthurian revival which is actually played out, as in the case of Edward I and other Arthurian imitators, and the literary ideal of chivalry which we encounter in Malory or Spenser. Malory has too often been identified with the antiquarian tastes of his first printer, Caxton, whose interest in chivalry did not go much beyond the accoutrements of chivalric rituals. Malory's revival of chivalry, on the other hand, must have seemed to him appropriate to the political and cultural interests of his time. We can not hope to understand the thematic significance of *Le Morte Darthur* unless we can learn to make a new distinction between nostalgia and revival. Rosemond Tuve makes this distinction on behalf of Tudor interest in romances, and it is certainly equally applicable to Malory. Nostalgia in romance literature, she says, involves a "recreation of what

is lost, a harking back and wishful return to a vanished past,''
and is characteristic of nineteenth- and twentieth-century
Arthurian revivals and not of Spenser.[17] In this respect the
only difference between Malory and a writer like Spenser is
that each chose to revive Arthurian romance for different
reasons. Spenser did not attempt a full scale application of
the Arthurian legend to figure forth his ideas, and consequently he did not run into the same problems with the
legend that Malory encountered.

Although a study of this kind is primarily concerned with
the thematic structure of the book, it is not possible to do
justice to Malory's themes without employing both source
study and structural analysis as well. As a consequence, in
analyzing the book we must pay very close attention to Malory's handling of his sources. This kind of study reveals
the author's conscious attempts to manipulate the story to
suit his own ends; at the same time one is forced to recognize
in Malory's narrative the growing disparity between his views
and the direction in which the narrative is destined to move.
Structurally, too, any rearrangement of the narrative was
bound to reveal a great deal about the nature of the source
as Malory understood it. Too much scholarship has assumed
that Malory read the Vulgate Cycle and his other Arthurian
sources with the same understanding of them as we have.
Both source study and structural analysis reveal that this
may not have been the case. But, although the meaning of
Malory's book stands independent of source study, it is a
useful way of checking up on one's critical assumptions.

The discussion of political theory which follows will be a
constant point of reference for the thematic study of *Le
Morte Darthur* in the next two chapters. Here it is simply
intended to provide some clues as to Malory's probable political expectations in dealing with the Arthurian story.

Fifteenth-century English political thought does not show
a sharp break from the political theory of the earlier cen-

17. Rosemond Tuve, *Allegorical Imagery: Some Mediaeval Books and
Their Posterity* (Princeton, 1966), p. 340.

turies of the Middle Ages. It does, however, show a different
focus of attention which emphasizes and utilizes one aspect
of earlier English political theory to the exclusion of much
else. The nature and limits of the king's sacred authority
and his relation to the polity are the crucial problems for
fifteenth-century jurists. Their concern seems to stem from
a sense of what we might loosely call "nationalism." They
are anxious to define what characterizes England as a nation
and to determine what or who comprises this nation, as well
as to establish for posterity the means by which the "nation"
will perpetuate itself. The issue of kingship and its relation
to law is at the center of the problem as they see it.

As Ernst Kantorowicz has shown, the "political theology"
of the King's Two Bodies which reached its fullest statement
in the fifteenth century and received its most extensive application later during the Tudor monarchy was a product of a
long tradition in English political thought. Before analyzing
three figures who illustrate the most important aspects of this
tradition, I shall summarize Kantorowicz' work on the subject. If I seem to be following slavishly the interpretations
and findings of Kantorowicz it is because my readings in
medieval political theory have reinforced my acceptance of
his conclusions. What I have added—besides pinpointing
specific issues relating to Malory in John of Salisbury (ca.
1115–1180), Bracton (ca.1210–1268), and Fortescue (ca.1394–
1476)—is some indication of what the fiction of the King's
Two Bodies suggests about the social and cultural tensions of
the time.

The origins of this peculiarly English theory of kingship
are theological, and the parallel between the church and the
state and that between Christ and king must not be forgotten
when we come to Malory. Christ's double nature is the model
for the king's twinned person. As the theory developed and
expanded from its theological background the king was assigned a mortal and an immortal body: a natural or private
person and a public person corresponding to the body politic.
The parallel between the king's double nature and the *per-*

sona mixta of the christological thinking carries over to the analogy between church and state as well: ''It is evident that the doctrine of theology and canon law, teaching that the Church, and Christian society in general, was a *'corpus mysticum* the head of which is Christ' has been transferred by the jurists from the theological sphere to that of the state the head of which is the king.[18]

It is essential to understand that the King's Two Bodies are inseparable in life. They have, or ought to have, different functions and areas of influence, but the king's natural body is forever joined to his superbody through his anointment and consecration. Furthermore, the inseparability of natural body and body politic provides a way of explaining how the office transforms the man: ''the body politic contains mysterious forces which remove the imperfections of the body natural.''[19] The effect of the theory is to identify the mortal with the immortality of his office or body politic; the king is therefore paradoxically immortal in time. The mysterious way in which the king participates in immortality without actually being immortal is clarified by the explanation of the king's death or ''demise,'' which is at the heart of the fifteenth-century interpretations of the political fiction. At the time of the king's death the immortal part of kingship, the king's body politic, is removed from his body natural and transferred to that of his successor. Thus the continuity of political forms is secured, and their sacred character is not impaired by the mortality of a single individual.

The first explicit statements of this kind on the meaning of the king's death appeared in the fifteenth century around the time of the Wars of the Roses. This phenomenon is easily explained by the fact that the frequent changes of monarchs prompted jurists to formulate a theory which would demonstrate the immortality of the office despite fluctuations in its occupants, and to show that the character of the English ''nation'' is not damaged or altered by a change in monarch:

18. Kantorowicz, *King's Two Bodies*, p. 14.
19. *Ibid.*, p. 9.

"each transfer of power from Lancaster to York and back was legally interpreted as the *demise* of the defeated king."[20] The matter of treason too was easily accounted for in these terms. Treason is an attack on the king's natural body which cannot damage his immortal body politic.

This double nature of kingship and its connection with immortality is based upon a time scheme or an understanding of time which is significantly different from the Augustinian duality of Time and Eternity of the early Middle Ages. The Augustinian view emphasized the inferior nature of Time which was totally dissociated from Eternity and therefore "doomed to meet an abrupt end at any given moment."[21] Clearly the apocalyptic character of this view would render any speculations on the permanence of human institutions incomprehensible.

The nation of *aevum*, a time series which occupies a middle ground between Time and Eternity, and therefore between man and God, liberated medieval thought from the Augustinian duality. The relevance of the recovery of *aevum* to this discussion of the theory of the King's Two Bodies becomes apparent as soon as one realizes that the apocalyptic thinking of the Augustinian view was hereby replaced with a sense of the infinite continuity of the world. "*Aevum* was a kind of infiniteness and duration which had motion and therefore past and future, a sempiternity which according to all authorities was endless."[22] *Aevum* was also the time series occupied by the angels. Similarly, the immortal body of the king, his body politic, was also located in the time sphere of the angels and for that reason fifteenth-century jurists contrived the concept of the king's *character angelicus*. By associating the body politic with the holy spirits and angels the jurist at once gave it a sacred nature and also demonstrated that like the angels it figured forth the immutable within time.

20. *Ibid.*, p. 13n.
21. *Ibid.*, p. 275.
22. *Ibid.*, p. 279.

These are the theoretical notions or "fictions" which formed the background for the legalistic thinking about the limits and nature of kingship. Both the notion of *aevum*, or continuity, and the christological parallel of the twinned nature of the king must be kept in mind as we look at the application of this fiction in discussions of the king's relation to law, questions of nationalism, and tyranny, and the functions and attitudes appropriate to either the public or the private person of the king.

The first thing that strikes one about the implications of the fiction of the King's Two Bodies as it reached its formulation in the fifteenth century, is the strongly constitutional bent which the term "body politic," or "mystical body," assumes. One begins to suspect that not only was the fiction designed to assure the continuity of kingship, but that it was also intended as a way of establishing a limited monarchy. In the fifteenth century, therefore, the "body politic" was no longer defined simply as the king's person in his official or public capacity, but as a corporation: the actual body had the king for its head and his subjects as members.

It is interesting that Kantorowicz found no Continental antecedent or parallel to this physiological metaphor of the state as a human body. The significance of the metaphor as a way of limiting the monarchy is easily seen: just as the King's Two Bodies were inseparable except in death, the body politic could not be divided into head and limbs or it would cease to function as a body. By the fifteenth century, as we shall see in the writings of Fortescue, the king's public capacity was conveniently defined as: "a body politic which was not separated from either its royal constituent as the head nor from those co-responsible for the *status coronae* as limbs. Who those limbs were depended upon the occasion: they were sometimes the councillors, sometimes the magnates, and sometimes the Lords together with the Commons in Parliament."[23]

The fifteenth-century definition of the crown is very closely

23. *Ibid.*, p. 382.

related to this metaphor of the state as a human body. In the later fifteenth century the crown was continually spoken of as public property belonging to both king and subjects. The public nature of the crown furthermore extends to the *Dignitas* of the king's *persona idealis*: the king's dignity, his regal rights, never die. The constitutional trend which we have been following in political theory culminated in this ideal of the crown which is at the service of the common good: "It [the crown] was something that touched all and, therefore, was 'public,' and no less public than waters, highways or *fiscus*. It served the common utility and thus was superior to both the king and the lords spiritual and secular including —a little later—the commons as well.'"[24] Now the whole thrust of this tradition of medieval political thought becomes clear: the twinned person of the king is designed to assure the continuity of his office; his public person is inseparable from the advisory body of which it is the head. From this we see that both the continuity of the royal office and its close relation with the subjects it rules are theories designed to put kingship at the service of the common good.

The perpetuation of the crown and the crown's devotion to public utility or the common good are the central propositions in fifteenth-century England. Law was declared the means by which both of these goals were to be achieved. Jurists established the sacred and immortal nature of the law by again borrowing from ecclesiastical terminology. The king is to the law as the priest is to the sacrament.[25] The king is therefore a priest of the law, and his immortality is hereby accounted for because he is the representative of the immortal idea of justice. The concept of the prince as a living model of the law was not new in the fifteenth century or even in the twelfth century, but it received special emphasis in the fifteenth century because, according to contemporary jurists, it was the law which would assure the immortality of the body politic.

24. *Ibid.*, p. 362.
25. *Ibid.*, pp. 134ff.

The highly theoretical and fictional nature of this background material is tempered somewhat when it is illustrated by the writings of Salisbury, Bracton, and Fortescue. By taking them in chronological order one can see what aspects of an earlier tradition of political theory were retained and emphasized in Malory's time.

John of Salisbury's *Policraticus* (1129) contains many of the ideas which were to influence political thought in the fifteenth and sixteenth centuries.[26] The emphasis throughout the work is upon the idea of justice, and John employs the metaphor of the prince as both the image of God and the image of immortal justice. Law is the external means by which justice is perpetuated, but the prince is its living exemplar. It is important to recognize that in describing kingship John does not dwell upon the king's knowledge of the law or on the legal aspects of his office. He stresses instead the king's role as a model whose behavior is dictated by an innate sense of equity.[27] We find this idea again in Fortescue's advice to the prince in his *De Laudibus Legum Angliae.*

John's theory of the prince as the image of justice is based on his contrast between the true prince as the image of equity and the tyrant as the image of depravity, which was very influential in subsequent treatises on monarchy.[28] The contrast draws upon the theory of the King's Two Bodies to make its point. There is an antithesis between the *persona publica* of the prince and his *privata voluntas*; the tyrant is the ruler who is guided in his public decisions by his private whims or interests.[29]

The severity of John's comments on tyranny and the frequency with which they are introduced stem from his under-

26. John Dickinson, ''The Medieval Conception of Kingship as Developed in the *Policraticus* of John of Salisbury,'' *Speculum*, I (1926), 308. Dickinson establishes the influence of the *Policraticus* on later medieval political theory.

27. John of Salisbury, *Policraticus*, ed. C. J. Webb (Oxford, 1909), IV, 2ff.

28. *Ibid.*, III, 15ff.

29. *Ibid.*, IV, 2. See also Kantorowicz, *King's Two Bodies*, p. 96.

lying assumption about the function of the state which the prince represents.[30] He treats both prince and law in sacred terms because they are the guardians of ''the spiritual and ethical elements orienting social life.''[31] The state, therefore, has a moral and sacred purpose to perpetuate the immortal idea of Justice which the tyrant must not be at liberty to disturb. By describing the tyrant as an image of depravity, John emphasizes the antithesis between the deterioration of the state in his hands and its perpetuation in the hands of the true prince.

Here the guiding concern is for the public utility, or common interest, for which the king is responsible. The king's acts are not his own; they are acts for the community which he represents.[32] But there is an important distinction to be made between John's statements on the king's *persona publica* and the constitutionalist thinking which characterizes the fifteenth-century definitions of the king's body politic. John insists that the king owes his authority to his appointment by God; he represents the commonwealth and is responsible for it, but he does not have to answer *to* it. He does not hold his office from the people.

John's state, therefore, is not formed by social contract. It is created by God and ruled through him by the prince. The *persona publica* is not framed by the policy making of men, although it is concerned with their welfare. Furthermore, Dickinson, in his appraisal of the whole of the *Policraticus*, can find no indication ''that the community can organize itself for the accomplishment of its common purposes by developing institutions for pooling the ideas and harmonizing the ends of its members.''[33] Tyranny, as John recognized, is not the sole prerogative of the king. Some of the king's subjects by virtue of their superior position were bound to tyrannize others. The state, and consequently the strong

30. John of Salisbury, *Policraticus*, VII, 11.
31. W. Ullmann, ''Influence of John of Salisbury,'' *English Historical Review*, LIX (1944), 390.
32. John of Salisbury, *Policraticus*, IV, 1.
33. Dickinson, ''Medieval Conception of Kingship,'' p. 336.

position of the prince in *Policraticus*, exists to protect the members from this kind of tyranny.[34]

This skepticism seems distinctly out of keeping with the constitutional ideal of the fifteenth century. What is interesting is that John makes the very distinction between regal rule and political rule that Fortescue later adopted to praise the English form of government. John's definition of the two kinds of government has a different twist to it from that of his successor, however. Like Fortescue he holds that political rule is the ideal form of government—that is, government by law or by peers which is to be distinguished from strictly regal government. But he adds that this is an ideal which is not appropriate to man in a state of sin; it presumes too much from human nature and is only suitable to man in a state of innocence. Nevertheless, Book VIII, 17 shows the author's inclination to wish for a condition of innocence which would allow men to participate in government by social contract. What John held out as a desirable but unrealizable goal had become by the fifteenth century a "realistic" ambition according to Fortescue. What is important here is that the proposition of political rule remained the political ideal in the English imagination, despite John's warnings about its dangers.

There are a number of complications relating to the interpretation of Bracton's *De Legibus et Consuetudinibus Angliae* (1259), which make it difficult for the non-specialist to say that Bracton held this or that position on questions of kingship and government.[35] There is in fact little agreement among scholars about the meaning of Bracton's most important statements on kingship and its relation to the law. What is ascertainable, however, is the nature of the problems which Bracton placed in the most prominent position in his writings. Although his final decision on a particular prob-

34. John of Salisbury, *Policraticus*, VIII, 17.
35. Fritz Schulz, "Bracton on Kingship," *English Historical Review*, LX (1945), 136–76. Schulz illustrates the complications in interpreting Bracton's theories of kingship.

lem may not be clear, it is possible to show what problems attracted his attention and subsequently that of Malory's contemporaries.

It is perhaps surprising that as a jurist Bracton focuses less upon the fine distinctions of legal procedure than upon the nature of kingship. He treats many of the problems which we found in John of Salisbury, and there is the same concern throughout his works for the perpetuation of justice and peace and for the continuity of the state or *fisc* which outlives the individual king. As in John of Salisbury, the ideal of peace and the liquidation of tyranny remain the goals of government. Bracton has taken these issues farther, however, until we see that peace and tyranny form the central dichotomy of his political theory by which all governments can be judged.

To begin with, Bracton seems as conservative as John in his statements on the king's position as the vicar of God from whom he takes his power. But the significance of Bracton's insistence upon the sacred nature of kingship involves more than simply making the king answerable only to God. Through emphasizing the sacred nature of kingship, Bracton established the sacred character of the state and the things belonging to the state such as the ''King's Peace'' and the ''King's Justice.''[36] Bracton borrowed terminology from the church and argued that, ''A thing quasi-sacred is a thing fiscal which cannot be given away or be sold or transferred upon another person by the prince or ruling king; and those things make the crown what it is, and they regard to the common utility such as peace and justice.''[37]

Here is the same emphasis on the king's obligation to the commonweal that we found in John of Salisbury; again the ideal of peace through law is the king's way of serving the commonweal. Peace and justice are sacred things belonging

36. Henry of Bracton, *De legibus et consuetudinibus Angliae*, ed. G. E. Woodbine (New Haven, 1915–1942), II, 57ff.
37. Kantorowicz, *King's Two Bodies*, p. 173. This quotation is Kantorowicz's translation of Bracton, *De legibus*, II, 58.

to the public person of the king; they are therefore eternal and can not be given away or transferred by the king. In dealing with the sacramental character of the state, the king's office, and the law which maintains them, Bracton frequently resorts to the maxim *Nullum tempus currit contra regem,* "Time runneth not against the king," demonstrating that his overriding concern is with the perpetuation of these sacred things in time.[38] The obligation of government, then, is to assure peace by providing a future for itself.

There is an interesting sidelight to Bracton's deification of the immortal *fisc,* or state, which represented for him both prince and *patria.* It is not coincidental that the fifteenth-century extensions of Bracton's tendency to turn the *fisc* into something quasi-holy took on a strongly nationalistic tone.[39] This aspect of later medieval political theory had its roots in the use of ecclesiastical terminology to describe the immortal nature of the state and the semi-religious devotion appropriate to it. Although it has lost some of its religious overtones, the "nationalism" of Fortescue's *De Laudibus Legum Angliae* and indeed of Malory's *Morte Darthur* seems to be a direct outgrowth of this kind of thinking, and is not therefore to be understood as nationalistic in strictly modern terms.

Although Bracton describes the king as the vicar of God, he also dwells at length upon the king's relation and obligation to the law. The king is not above the law. Throughout Bracton's work there is the insistence that once the king asserts his private will in opposition to the "immortal law" his actions become those of a tyrant. Furthermore, according to the Bracton scholar Schulz, the king "who violates his duty to maintain justice automatically *ceases to be king;* his acts are void because they are not in truth acts of a king."[40] As Schulz points out, these statements and indeed all of Bracton's comments on kingship have as their center

38. Bracton, *De legibus,* II, 293.
39. Kantorowicz, *King's Two Bodies,* p. 189.
40. Schulz, "Bracton on Kingship," p. 153.

the coronation oath of the English king. This legal speculation on justice and tyranny as they relate to the coronation
oath becomes one of the most significant parts of English
political theory in the fifteenth century.

Bracton's constitutionalist qualification of the king's power
to make law allows for a larger measure of control on the
part of the king's council than does John of Salisbury. According to Bracton, the king can not make laws arbitrarily,
or by personal whim, but only with the aid and deliberation
of his council.[41] Consequently, the relation of the king to
his immediate council and his choice of members for it are
central concerns of fourteenth- and fifteenth-century legal
thought. There is an obvious trend in Bracton away from
the strictly regal rule of the *Policraticus*. The issue at hand
is very closely related to the late medieval concern with the
continuity of the realm which manifested itself in the constitutional struggles of the fourteenth century. The growing
importance of the king's council indicates the barons' awareness that "things of a public nature no longer touched the
king alone, but touched the king as well as the whole realm."[42]
What has happened by the end of Bracton's age, then, is that
legal theorists have demonstrated the crucial difference between the king as a personal liege lord with feudal or private
obligations to certain members of the realm and the king "as
a supra-individual administrator of a public sphere—a
public sphere which included the *fisc* that never died."[43]

Before turning to the uses which the fifteenth century
found for the political tradition of John of Salisbury and
Bracton, we must examine the background and contemporary
meaning of the English coronation oath in some detail. As
Mr. Schulz demonstrates in his article, "Bracton on Kingship," the coronation oath of the English king is central to
everything Bracton says about kingship.[44] The same thing is

41. Bracton, *De legibus*, II, 305.
42. Kantorowicz, *King's Two Bodies*, p. 190.
43. *Ibid.*, p. 191.
44. Schulz, "Bracton on Kingship," p. 145.

true of Fortescue's *De Laudibus Legum Angliae,* and, in fact, the oath was at the center of the controversy over the deposition of Edward II and Richard II.

The essentials of the English coronation oath are set forth by Percy Schramm in his *History of the English Coronation Oath.* The three *praecepta* which formed the original oath call for the king to preserve peace, remove wrongdoing, and establish justice.[45] Despite the sketchiness of such promises this formula remained essentially unchanged down to the time of Bracton, when the inadequacy of the oath as a means of binding the king to the realm became a major issue. Even in its most primitive form the English coronation oath is characterized by its insistence on the king's obligations to his people, although early medieval English kings were not always constrained to see the oath in this way.

In the late thirteenth century, when the inadequacies of the oath became a major concern, the jurists and chroniclers filled out the three meager statements with their own interpretations of what the promises implied: ''1) the preservation of peace together with the protection of Church and clergy, 2) the maintenance of good laws and the abolition of bad ones, 3) the equitable administration of justice to all men.''[46] Besides these interpretations, further suggestions were made for the modification of the oath, such as the ones in the law book *Leges Anglorum saeculi XIII inuentis collectae* where the author suggested the following additions: ''the property of the Crown cannot be alienated; if alienated it must be recovered; the king must rule *rite,* that is to say according to law, and not according to his own will nor arbitrarily, but *per iudicium proceruum regni.*''[47] These two suggestions form the keynote of the modified oath of 1308.

In 1308 Edward II took a coronation oath modeled on the three *praecepta* but sworn in the manner of answers to direct

45. Percy Schramm, *A History of the English Coronation Oath* (Oxford, 1947), pp. 18ff.

46. *Ibid.,* p. 196.

47. *Ibid.*

questions which bound him to specific laws. In addition a
fourth item bound the king to observe not only past legislation but also the future legislation enacted by his subjects.
During his reign the coronation oath was used repeatedly by
Parliament to compel the king to act for the benefit of the
people. On the issue of Gaveston, the king's favorite, Parliament put forth a declaration stating that the oath distinguished between the Crown and the person of the king:
that is between the king's private person and the public
benefits of the kingdom, and therefore in a matter such as
that of Gaveston the king was bound to renounce his private
interests when they interfered with the commonweal.[48] This
interpretation carried great weight in the fifteenth century
when jurists like Fortescue stated quite boldly that the meaning of the coronation oath, despite protests to the contrary,
signified the king's acknowledgment that he was *under* the
law.

The central issues concerning kingship and the law found
in John of Salisbury and Bracton are further refined and
emphasized in Sir John Fortescue's *De Laudibus Legum
Angliae*. This fifteenth-century work announces itself as a
treatise on law, but, as in Fortescue's predecessors, law can
only be meaningfully discussed in its relation to the office
of kingship. Fortescue's work is more than anything else
a handbook on the proper relationship between king and law,
and in fact it was written for the benefit of Prince Edward.
In his preface Fortescue makes clear that the lesson of the
Wars of the Roses prompted this tract on kingship and that
his work is intended as a corrective for the late abuses and
misapplications of the king's political role. Because it was
written at what the author considered a time of political
crisis when the traditions of English government were in
danger of being subverted, the book is an especially clear
and emphatic statement of the most crucial issues of late
medieval English political theory.

Through law, or rather through the English form of law,

48. *Ibid.*, p. 197.

the perpetuation of the mystical body of the state is assured. Fortescue discusses law as the instrument for the attainment of justice—that sacred virtue which stabilizes and perpetuates civilization. The king as keeper of the law—and this is his primary role—performs what Fortescue calls a "sacred function," and there is consequently a holy sanction for his acts.[49] By its very nature law is the agent of stability because it is not changeable or adaptable at the whim of individuals. Fortescue continually emphasizes that law is "the art of what is good and equal."[50] In his instructions to the prince he stresses that the king as keeper of the law is not necessarily bound to be knowledgeable about specific aspects of actual laws, but he is the keeper of the idea of law—of justice itself. As we saw in John of Salisbury the king is a model of justice —a kind of living law. The significance of the king's role is best understood through Fortescue's definition of law and justice: "Human laws are no other than rules whereby the perfect notion of justice can be determined: but that justice, which those laws discover, is not of the commutative, or distributive kind, or any one particular distinct virtue, but it is *virtue absolute and perfect.*"[51] The king in his public person is the model of this kind of justice. He is the exemplar of this virtue which the laws of his kingdom are intended to maintain.

Fortescue's idealism concerning the king's role goes far beyond what we have seen in John of Salisbury and Bracton while at the same time continuing in their tradition. The old distinction between regal and political rule which appears in the *Policraticus* is at the center of *De Laudibus Legum Angliae.* Political rule, which John had defined as the province of man in a state of innocence, is according to Fortescue the kind of government which the laws of England have created. Nevertheless, Fortescue does not deny the highly

49. Sir John Fortescue, *De Laudibus Legum Angliae,* trans. Francis Gregor (London, 1917), p. 5.

50. *Ibid.*

51. *Ibid.,* Chapter IV.

idealistic nature of such a system; it is just this which appeals to his sense of his country's greatness. In speaking of the mixed political and regal rule which prevails in England he comments, "With such a law, saith the same St. Thomas, all mankind would have been governed, if, in the Paradise, they had not transgressed the command of God."[52] It is easy to see the appeal which this visionary system had for an age torn by civil strife and anxious to reaffirm established traditions of kingship and law. Fortescue's conception of king and polity may be no more ideal or idealistic than that of his predecessors, but he is advertising it as such in order to convince his contemporaries of its worth and of the crucial importance of maintaining it. This is the real function of such idealistic language, and—as we shall see—it is also characteristic of Malory's didactic approach to the political themes of the Arthurian story.

The distinction between regal rule and political rule is the distinction between "rule by mere arbitrary will and pleasure of the king over the people" and rule which originates in a social contract totally devoted to the common good or common utility.[53] Regal rule by itself is characteristic of the government of France, and Fortescue takes great pains whenever he can to contrast the French and English systems of government to the detriment of the former. The danger of regal government, besides the potentially arbitrary nature of the king's decision making, is that it cannot work for the common good because it does not protect the individual from the malice of his enemies. In describing the legal customs of such a country Fortescue leads the prince to conclude that "a man who lives under such a government . . . lives exposed to frequent hazards of this sort: enemies are designing and desperately wicked."[54] The purpose of government and the role of the king, then, according to Fortescue are to assure the safety of the individual and consequently

52. *Ibid.*, p. 18.
53. *Ibid.*, p. 20.
54. *Ibid.*, p. 46.

the stability of the realm. Fortescue's concern with these issues is proportionate to the threats of instability and tyranny in his time.

Like Bracton, Fortescue centers all of his commentary on the king's mixed political capacity as public and private person around the English coronation oath. It is constantly in his mind in Chapters XXXV and XXXVI, when he is comparing the monarchies of England and France. The regal government of France does not demand that the king divide his *privata voluntas* from his *persona publica*; thus the king is left in absolute authority over his people. Fortescue is very quick to point out that a king's dignity is not vested in the degree of his power but in his identification of his public person with the common good. Paradoxically the absolute king suffers a loss of dignity by virtue of his omnipotence: "to be able to do mischief, which is the sole prerogative an absolute prince enjoys above the other, is so far from increasing his power, that it rather lessens and exposes it."[55] The incipient nationalism in earlier medieval English legal thinkers is virtually unchecked in Fortescue; he has taken both the idealism and the patriotic tendencies of these thinkers to an extreme in order to counteract the disillusionment of his time. Many of the aspects of his distinctions between the regal rule of France and the mixed political and regal rule of England are the same contrasts and parallels which Malory creates between the reigns of Uther and Arthur, and between the governments of Arthur and Mark.

Before examining the evidence of contemporary political issues in Malory's book, we need to see what Fortescue meant by the mystical body politic and how he defined it for his contemporaries. The body politic as Fortescue describes it must not be defined by the king's public person alone, but by the king plus his council and parliament. According to Chapter XII, England's mission is to become the successor to Rome and Israel as the living example of the ideal mixed regal and political government. The government is defined

55. *Ibid.*, p. 24.

by reference to the physiological metaphor of the human body. Fortescue quotes Augustine, who says "that a people is a body of men joined together in society by a consent of right, by a union of interests, and for promoting the common good." To this Fortescue adds that such an assemblage can not be considered a political body until it has a head:

Wherefore, it is absolutely necessary, where a company of men combine and form themselves into a *body politic*, that some one should preside as the governing principal, who goes usually under the name of *king*.

In this order, as out of an embrio, is formed an human body, with one head to govern and control it; so from a confused multitude is formed a regular kingdom, which is a sort of a mystical body, with one person, as the head, to guide and govern.[56]

Fortescue's polity-centered kingship is held together by law. The metaphor outlined above is extended to describe law as the ligament by which the body politic is bound together in a whole. We easily see by now that the entire physiological metaphor is in fact a metaphor of unity and continuity—the two overriding concerns of fifteenth-century politics. Furthermore, out of this metaphor of the body politic (king and council as head and body) emerged the idea of the *regnum as patria*—an object of political devotion akin to the religious devotion due the Church.[57] When readers discern a nationalistic bias in Malory's *Morte Darthur* they are not wrong: this quasi-religious devotion to the *patria* is an integral part of his design for Arthur and the Round Table.

Once the major characteristics of fifteenth-century political thought and its backgrounds are set forth, we may examine their relationship to the Arthurian story as Malory saw it. The exact evidence of these political theories at work in the book will appear in the tale-by-tale analysis of the book in Chapters 3 and 4. At present I am concerned with showing why Malory may have seized upon the Arthurian story as a

56. *Ibid.*, p. 21.
57. Kantorowicz, *King's Two Bodies*, p. 232.

vehicle for his political morality—what there is about the story that enabled him to set it up in the first tales with the trappings of political idealism. In such an analysis one must make a distinction between what Malory adds to the story to fit his probably preconceived notions about it, and what it already contained that may have attracted his attention to it in the first place. The latter point engages me here.

As we have seen in the intensely patriotic writings of Fortescue, England had become in the eyes of certain jurists the new Rome, the incarnation of that immortal justice which had previously been the province of Rome. This idea of England's mission was very easily attached to the Arthurian story, since earlier English versions like Geoffrey's *Historia Regum Britanniae* and the late fourteenth-century alliterative *Morte Arthure* had already established the Arthurian story as, in part, a record of England's triumphant succession to the position of Rome. Malory's interest in exploiting this aspect of the native Arthurian tradition is easily seen in his "Tale of Arthur and the Emperor Lucius," where he gives special emphasis to the Roman campaign and enlarges Arthur's role as emperor of a new Rome.

Apart from this idea of the mission of England, there are of course other nationalistic elements in the Arthurian story. To Geoffrey the history of Britain is nowhere more glorious than during the reign of Arthur. For this reason he gives his history a three-part structure of birth, flowering, and decay, placing the Arthurian section in the central position. Geoffrey's gift to the native tradition of Arthurian legend is this nationalistic coloring of the story. Everything in British history, according to his text, leads up to the reign of Arthur; and all that follows is civil strife and subjection to foreign invaders: "Thereafter for many ages did the Britons lose the crown of the kingdom and the sovereignty of the island, nor made they any endeavour to recover their former dignity."[58] Contrast this statement with the national-

58. Geoffrey of Monmouth, *History of the Kings of Britain*, trans. Sebastian Evans (New York, 1958), XI, 11, p. 241.

istic fervor of the Arthurian chapters, where soldiers are instructed to die for their country as they would die for their religion: ''Fight ye therefore for your country, and if it be that death overtake ye, suffer it willingly for your country's sake, for death itself is victory and healing unto the soul, inasmuch as he that shall have died for his brethren doth offer himself a living sacrifice unto God.''[59]

The Arthurian story must have appeared to the native Englishman as the one brilliant episode in British history divided off from the episodes of disunity, tyranny, or invasion which preceded and followed it. We can for the moment disregard the causes of Arthur's downfall, since in the English tradition of Geoffrey they are largely external rather than internal. Looked at in this way, the story most likely appealed to Malory as the ideal embodiment for the patriotic notions of his own time—notions also born out of experiences similar to those which surrounded the Arthurian story: civil wars, threats of tyranny, and foreign wars.

Many other parts of the Arthurian story at first glance make it seem an appropriate vehicle for the political moralizing of Malory's time. The very idea of Arthur's Round Table contains potential similarities to the physiological metaphor of the state as a human body with the king as the head and his councilors as limbs. The Round Table is metaphorically the body of which Arthur is the head, and Malory takes every opportunity to bring the relationships and obligations of the Round Table into line with the central political metaphor of his own age. Geoffrey invested the Arthurian legend with a special significance; to him the reign of Arthur represented the first unification of the whole island in British history. The Arthurian legend as a unification myth obviously corresponds very nicely to the political metaphor of the mystical body which was also designed as a fiction of unity. It will be evident in Chapter 3 that Malory changed and added to his sources to portray the Round Table and its relationship to the king and the realm along

59. *Ibid.*, IX, 4, pp. 187–88.

these lines. Malory's additions to the earlier versions of the story underline over and over again that his major concern is with the function and the importance of Arthur's fellowship as a means of unifying and governing the country.

Arthurian society certainly looks as though it fits Fortescue's definitions of the mystical body or body politic, and Malory must have so viewed it. It had from its very inception strong christological associations which would reinforce the notions of the sacred nature of the state that characterize medieval political theory. Although little or no mention has been made of these associations in Malory criticism, we should not assume that Malory himself was unaware of their implications. The primary religious association in Malory's book is that between Arthur and his Round Table and Christ and his apostles. Laura Hibbard Loomis has written very convincingly about the origins of the Round Table in Christian art.[60] She shows that there was an unbroken tradition in the religious art of Wace's Normandy which depicted Christ and the apostles sitting at a round table for the Last Supper. Because round tables were virtually unknown in daily medieval life, Mrs. Loomis concludes that Arthur's round table probably had religious origins and associations. Since these associations were not lost on the authors of the Vulgate Arthurian romances, they most likely were known to Malory as well.

Other parallels between Arthur and Christ and between the Round Table and the Church can be established with more certainty. Edmund Reiss has noticed that the dates assigned for the feats which establish Arthur as the true king are all holy days marking significant and parallel events in the life of Christ: "At the Feast of the Epiphany on January 6—traditionally the holy day celebrating the Manifestation of Christ's glory—Arthur repeats the significant act that reveals his presence in the world. Again he is called upon to remove the sword at Candlemas, February 2—the Feast

60. Laura Hibbard Loomis, ''Arthur's Round Table,'' *Publications of the Modern Language Association*, XLI (1926), 771–84.

of the Purification and the climax of the rites celebrating the Incarnation of Christ—and again at Easter—the holy day celebrating the Resurrection. . . . .'"[61] Most important, however, is the last occasion upon which Arthur draws the sword from the stone—the Feast of the Pentecost. At this point the commons claim Arthur for their king; thus the parallel between Pentecost, the descent of the Holy Spirit to establish the Church, and the coming of Arthurian society is made clear. Reiss sees all of these associations as evidence that the Arthurian story was meant to figure forth the birth of a new Christian society. This supposition is no doubt true, but as far as Malory's book is concerned there is a further significance. The christological parallels in the story are retained in Malory's version; they obviously reinforced for him the contemporary insistence that the state was both sacred and immortal.

It is not difficult to see how a fifteenth-century reader might have read into the Arthurian story the preoccupations of his own time. The matter of the king's twinned person may well have more than a tangential relationship to the figure of Arthur. As Kantorowicz shows, English political theology from the time of the Norman Anonymous to the late Tudor jurists saw the king as a being with two persons, "one descending from nature and the other from grace."[62] The royal superbody was joined to the king's natural body in some mysterious way. In his composition of Tale I, Malory cut and added to his text to bring out the same doubleness in Arthur's nature which peculiarly fitted him to be king. At first the mysterious birth of Arthur and the fact that he is predestined to be king look very like the joining of the natural body and the immortal body described in the fiction of the King's Two Bodies. Furthermore, the ideal of the king as the priest of the law or as the incarnation of law finds an apt parallel in the very structure of Arthurian romance, where Arthur is not himself the agent of justice but

61. Edmund Reiss, *Sir Thomas Malory* (New York, 1966), p. 38.
62. Kantorowicz, *King's Two Bodies*, p. 46.

the figure of justice for whom all equitable deeds are performed. An analysis of Tales III and IV shows that Malory deliberately makes this one of Arthur's roles clearer than it was in his sources. He consciously renders Arthur not so much an active king, but a ruler with an innate sense of justice.

Malory initially capitalizes on all the basic materials of Arthurian romance which seem to correspond to fifteenth-century political ideals. He adds and changes material in Book I to illustrate the public nature of Arthur's crown, which is at the service of common utility in contrast to the circumstance during the reign of Uther. Later he heightens the contrast between Arthur and Mark to display the distinction between political and regal rule which was traditional in medieval English political thought. He draws on the religious associations between Church and state to establish the sacred and immortal nature of the fellowship. These elements, and the bulk of the evidence which will be presented in Chapters 3 and 4, force one to ask why, if he had such propitious material at hand, did Malory refuse to display Arthurian society as the political and cultural ideal which his contemporaries believed it to be.

Any consideration of the religious overtones of Arthurian society brings us to the reason for its appeal to Malory's age. We have seen why its highly idealistic character seemed the perfect objective correlative for the idealistic mixed political and regal rule so crucial to a jurist like Fortescue. Malory may well have wished us to see Arthur initially as the messianic *rex justus* with all the christological overtones of the theory of the King's Two Bodies. But his choice of figures to represent this corporational ideal, Arthur and his Round Table, seems to have failed to fulfill this role for the very reasons that it at first appeared so promising. The history of Arthur's coming in Malory's sources and of the establishment of his fellowship is messianic indeed, but it also contains a degree of apocalypticism which means that because the whole structure was defined as an appendage to

Arthur's person it could not perpetuate or sustain itself independent of him. The only notion of the structure's immortality in the Arthurian story is the prophecy of Arthur's return. Unfortunately the ideal of *rex futurus* does not imply the kind of immortality essential to the theory of the King's Two Bodies. The nature of Arthurian society is such that it can have no progeny, and therefore it preserved itself with a myth of its own immortality: "Hic jacet Arthurus, rex quondam rex que futurus."

It is true that in Geoffrey, Wace, Layamon, and the alliterative *Morte* Constantine is named Arthur's legitimate heir. But none of these versions pretend that Constantine's reign is in any way a continuation of Arthur's. Wace emphasizes the connection between the death of Arthur, the destruction of the famed knights of the Round Table, and the complete collapse of Arthurian civilization. Wace's tone in the last sentence is quite revealing: he relates that Constantine did as he was bidden, held his lands well, but despite his efforts the Arthurian structure never reappeared. The belief in Arthur's return which Layamon states so poignantly is very obviously designed as a consolation for so great a loss. Constantine represents neither a continuation of the Arthurian world, nor a compensation for its end. He simply makes a perfunctory appearance in the various versions of Arthur's passing. Geoffrey is the most apocalyptic in his version of Arthur's fall. His entire history after Arthur's demise lives in the shadow of Arthurian greatness, and Merlin's grim prophecies (*Historia Regum Britanniae*, Book VII, Chap. 4) show the apocalypticism which underlies all the versions of the story which the *Historia* spawned.

The Arthurian story participates in a time scheme which is vastly different from Malory's own sense of time. The notion of *aevum* discussed earlier is not characteristic of the story in any of its earlier forms. As the structure of the narrative in the Vulgate romance shows, the world exists only in the present; there is no sense of succession or continuation, nor is there any indication that the events have a past and a future. Because the character of the Arthurian legend was formed by this Augustinian sense of time, it carries with it a kind of apocalypticism which was completely unsuitable for Malory's message. Malory was operating from a sense of time which assumed the continuance and succession of things, while his narrative material was structured by a sense of time characteristic of an earlier era. In his *Studies in Human Time* Georges Poulet describes the way in which the Christian of the early Middle Ages regarded himself in time. Poulet's description might apply equally well to the time sense of the Arthurian story in the Vulgate cycle: ''For the Christian of the Middle Ages the sense of his existence did not precede a sense of his continuance. He did not have first to discover himself existing in a present moment in order next to conceive himself as existing in time. For him, on the contrary, to feel that he existed was to feel himself to be: neither changing nor becoming nor in any way succeeding himself . . . [he made] no real distinction between existence and duration.''[63] As we have seen, late medieval political theories are predicated on the succession and continuance of human institutions and not upon the feeling that institutions existed in a present which was itself ephemeral. Everything in the Arthurian story, on the other hand, points to an indifference to the future and even towards a self-destructiveness which made it in the long run unadaptable as a model for fifteenth-century political theory.

On this matter of time, we shall see that Malory had a definite sense of an historical *past* of which Arthurian society is a part. He does not in any way regard the story as taking place in the eternal present. He constantly uses the phrase ''in tho days'' to indicate that he is examining the story as an historical ideal and is not trying to pass his book off as an allegorical record of his own times. The point of analyzing the two different time senses which the Arthurian story and Malory's version of it occupy is to explain why the story failed as an historical ideal but succeeded in the

63. Georges Poulet, *Studies in Human Time* (New York, 1956), p. 3.

end as an object lesson for Malory's age. To speak of a shift in the time sense from one age to another is simultaneously to speak of a pervasive shift in the values and attitudes of a culture.

As Malory's narrative progresses we uncover the fallaciousness of reviving the moral demands of one age, in this case the demands of a chivalric society, as a guide to another. For one thing, such a revival is accompanied by a sense of desperation arising as it does during a time of panic and potential governmental dissolution, and Malory's brief comments on his own times demonstrate this fact. In addition, there is a self-consciousness about the open advocacy of older moral demands which prevents them from being binding in a new cultural context. In the last three tables of *Le Morte Darthur* Malory seems to have become so aware of the price a society pays for the idealism and asceticism of chivalry that he can no longer treat chivalry as an historical ideal.

3

The "Historical Ideal of Life": Le Morte Darthur, Tales I–V

The profound inadequacy of Arthurian chivalry as an historical ideal of life and as a fictional vehicle to express fifteenth-century political concerns is the subject of Chapter 4. Before we can profitably examine the critique of Arthurian society implicit in *Le Morte Darthur*, it is necessary to provide evidence of fifteenth-century political theory at work in the book. My contention is that those contemporary emphases which Malory initially added to the story become, in the last tales, the very agents of his critique of Arthurian society. Although the Arthurian myth does bear certain resemblances to the crucial political issues of Malory's day, these resemblances eventually proved to be simply the external trappings of the story. It is evident in the last four tales that on the most profound level the Arthurian ideal could not survive Malory's moral scrutiny, nor could it justify the initial political investment which he made in it. The evidence of the first tales suggests that this final exposé of the Arthurian world in Tales VI–VIII was a planned part of the entire book.

The first part of this chapter deals with the thematic dimensions of Malory's structural changes in the story; the second involves a discussion of the genres employed in the book and examines how they too are used to construct the political framework of Malory's Arthurian ideal; the last and most extensive section examines the Arthurian ideal in the first five tales in the light of the medieval political theories outlined in the preceding chapter.

I

The political bias of Malory's book emerges almost as clearly from his structural techniques and his mixture of genres as it does from the specific thematic alterations of the narrative itself. Almost any alteration in the ordering of episodes is bound to affect their meaning. In Malory's case, the partial elimination of *entrelacement* as a narrative technique means that his version of the story does not create the atmosphere of a "perpetual present" characteristic of the French romances. Unlike the events in his sources, Malory's episodes are not and can not be extended indefinitely; they seem to be designed to exist in an historical and political context.

Vinaver wrongly believes that Malory's elimination of *entrelacement* indicates his desire to write separate episodes. Several tales and even separate episodes do in fact begin and/or end with a designation of the time of the action. Vinaver uses these time signatures as evidence that the author was supplying information about the event necessary for readers who would not have any other information concerning its historical context. On the contrary, however, these passages establish a definite over-all chronology; by answering the question of *when* a certain event took place, they supply a *reason* for its occurrence. The Balin story, for instance, is one of Vinaver's prime examples of an episode which is cut off from preceding and ensuing events by the author's opening comments, and by his elimination of *entrelacement* within

the narrative.[1] But, the Balin story is assigned to a particular time for a thematic reason. It begins with the following
information: "Afftir the deth of Uther regned Arthure, hys
son, which had grete warre in his dayes for to gete all Inglonde into hys honde; for there were many kyngis within
the realme of Inglonde and of Scotlonde, Walys and Cornu-
wayle" (44–45).[2]

The meaning of "The Knight with the Two Swords" in
Malory's version of it, depends on the fact that it occurs
before the establishment of the Round Table and *before* the
unification of the realm under Arthur. Furthermore, Malory
cut the episode off from its close connection with the Grail
quest, and by so doing gave it special political consequences.
We are meant to see in this story the internal problems of
government which the creation of the Round Table will presumably counteract. Malory's Balin story represents the political past of Arthurian society; this is a potentially self-
destructive structure in which the king has not yet established
a binding relationship between himself and his realm. Balin's
personal feud takes precedence over his loyalty and obligations to Arthur and to the welfare of the realm. By cutting
the Balin story off from the themes of the quest and assigning
it to a particular era in Arthurian history, Malory initiates
the chronological scheme which his narrative is to follow.
The French romances do not allow for a sense of narrative
development in time, but it is only through such development
in the *Le Morte Darthur* that we can both see the political
themes emerge and watch the Arthurian ideal undermine itself.

Balin's antisocial behavior, which prompts him to keep
the sword despite a severe warning, sets off a chain of events
which affects the community as a whole. Although he has
a strong *personal* loyalty to Arthur, emphasized in two

1. Eugene Vinaver (ed.), *The Works of Sir Thomas Malory* (Oxford, 1947), III, 1274.
2. This and all subsequent page references to *Le Morte Darthur* refer to Eugene Vinaver (ed.), *The Works of Sir Thomas Malory* (Oxford, 1954).

sourceless passages (49, 52), Balin's obligation clearly does not extend to the community of the court, or to the realm as a whole. Arthur at this point in time is not identifiable with his disunified and chaotic realm. Two alterations in the story make its political significance clear. First, Balin's "Dolorous Stroke" is ultimately a punishment for the anti-social behavior beginning with his revenge and exile, and not for his entrance into the Grail Chapel. Secondly, unlike the source, the prophecy that Balin will kill his brother is ful-filled, introducing the themes of fratricide & fatality which are so important for Malory's interpretation of later events. These two changes from the source emphasize the political consequences of disunity and of personal loyalties which thrive at the expense of the community. But even more im-portant, they relate the Balin story thematically to Merlin's two prophecies about political disorder and strife between members of the Round Table themselves (Tristram and Lancelot, Lancelot and Gawain) which Malory retains from his source. Finally, Malory's interest in the Balin story as a way of forecasting and introducing the problems of gov-ernment is again apparent in Merlin's prophecy at the end of the episode. In the source, Merlin's magical bridge tests only the bravery of the knights who would cross it, but Malory substitutes the pertinent moral condition that one must be "withoute treachery or vylany" to attempt the crossing (70).

In the fifteenth-century terms, a government perpetuates itself by defining the crown or the body politic in sufficiently public or corporate terms so that it is invulnerable to the private threats of villainy and treachery. Malory's narrative, as the end of the Balin story suggests, will examine the success of Arthurian society in its attempts to deal with this problem. The self-contained shape of the Balin episode and its historical position in the narrative allow it to figure forth in small the crucial governmental problem of *Le Morte Dar-thur*, and, indeed, of fifteenth-century political thought in general: how does the just government mediate between its public responsibilities to the common good and the private interests of its members?

I have used "The Knight with the Two Swords" as an example of the political significance of Malory's narrative structure because it introduces several characteristics of his narrative technique. First, the omission of the interlacing episodes which appear in the French prose cycle allows for the introduction of chronological time. The French romances, as Rosemond Tuve has shown, do give a sense of the progression of theme by allowing us to look at one theme or idea "through the perspective of several incidents."[3] They do not, however, provide any sense of the *advancement* of time. But Malory's themes depend very heavily upon a sense of historical time. It is essential that events in the development of Arthurian society be seen in a sequence in which their cause and effect can be made apparent. The Balin story carries its particular prefigurative meaning as a result of its place in Arthurian history. It stands between the episodes of civil war indicated in the opening lines of the story, and the formulation of the Round Table in the "Torre and Pelinor" section which immediately follows it.

Two further comments on the general nature of Malory's narrative structure reveal that those aspects of French narrative which he did retain work very well thematically. Miss Tuve's comments on the conventions of romance narrative in *Allegorical Imagery* point up the fact that these conventions are specifically suited to the structure of the quest. In a series of interlaced episodes in the French romances a knight, or knights, search out the true nature of some abstract quality, usually chastity, by pursuing its enemies.[4] The accumulation of such episodes pulls us in the direction of understanding the nature of that quality which is the subject of the quest. It is striking that Malory scholars have not noted that many of the major incidents in Malory's book are

3. Rosemond Tuve, *Allegorical Imagery: Some Medieval Books and Their Posterity* (Princeton, 1966), p. 364.
4. *Ibid.*, p. 345.

also very highly ordered according to these conventions of
the quest. The main difference between his narrative and
the kind Miss Tuve studies is that Malory uses parallel rather
than interlaced episodes to figure forth the abstraction in
question. This alteration gives his narrative both chronological time and a kind of dramatic action not open to the French
romance writer. Nevertheless, the affinity between the quest
conventions in the French romances and those in Malory is
very clear, although the thematic emphases differ sharply.
In *Le Morte Darthur* the quest is motivated by the desire to
perfect the nature of Arthurian society through chivalry:
the questing episodes therefore are most often designed to
search out the true nature of justice.

The most obvious, but by no means the only, extensive uses
of such parallel episodes occur in Tales III and IV. Both
Lancelot and Gareth are led through seemingly repetitive
episodes to confront the enemies of unity and justice who are
invariably characterized as being without mercy, brutal, and
envious of the Round Table. Each major episode in both
tales concludes with the offender's promise to present himself
to the Round Table at a future date, usually Pentecost. Each
of these "closed" episodes in these two tales, and also those
in the tales which follow them, functions as a moral vignette
concerning the threats to justice and stability. The outsiders
who must be subdued in countless passages early in the book,
and later the members of the Round Table themselves, are
always confronted with the same communal demand: they
are made to sacrifice their individual instincts so that no one
in the community is left at the mercy of brute force. We
must remember that at his coronation Arthur, in a sourceless passage (11), promises to restore justice and to right the
wrongs which occurred before his reign. Brute force, or the
tyranny of one individual over another, is the most per-
sistent external and internal threat to stability, as these parallel episodes reveal. I have chosen Tales III and IV to
exemplify the emergence of this theme, because they are
among Malory's most original pieces structurally. His re-

working of the narrative into a series of parallel episodes
underlines his concern for a government like the kind Fortescue advocates: one that does not leave a man exposed to
the tyranny of his enemies.

Certainly the addition of chronological time and the use
of parallel episodes emphasize the political themes of *Le Morte
Darthur*. In the thematic analysis of each tale I shall demonstrate in more detail exactly how this rearrangement of narrative structure allows certain themes to emerge and, in
fact, lays bare elements heretofore hidden in the Arthurian
story. Malory was bound to discover new thematic possibilities in the story once he eliminated the interlaced episodes
which to some degree camouflage the social and political structure underlying the Arthurian ideal.

One more structural characteristic peculiar to Malory is
noteworthy; critics have called it "retrospective narrative."[5]
This term was first used to account for the seeming lack of
unity in the book and the lapses in Malory's chronology.
Now that the case for unity is considered established, it is
time to consider the possible thematic dimension of the flash-
back technique. The chronological relationships in question
are those between Tales III and IV, and between IV and the
first sections of V. I have already indicated that the most
important structural relationship between III and IV is
that of their parallel episodes. Both tales are constructed
according to the conventions of the quest, and their episodes
are designed to reveal Arthurian society in pursuit of unity
and the nature of just government. There is no substantial
difference between the state of Arthurian society in IV from
that in III. Both tales belong to the same period in Arthurian
history, whereas the last sections of Tale V, "The Tale of
Tristram," represent a considerable distance in time from
the Gareth and Lancelot episodes. The reason for placing
Tale IV after Tale III, even though its events must have preceded those in III, is that the Gareth story represents Mal-

5. R. M. Lumiansky, "The Question of Unity in Malory's *Morte
Darthur*," *Tulane Studies in English*, V (1955).

ory's attempt to take the Arthurian ideal as it appears in the
tale of Lancelot and redesign it along more realistic lines.
There is consequently an advance in *theme* from III to IV,
although from Malory's point of view there is no advancement in *time*. Both stories could be assigned to the same
general era of Arthur's court. But since Tale IV forms a
commentary on Tale III, it is appropriately placed after the
Lancelot stories.

Similarly, the opening of Tale V brings us to a time in
Arthurian history which must be even earlier than that of
both Tales III and IV. Nevertheless, the structural relationship is again that of parallel episodes. Tristram is perform-
ing for Mark exactly those services which Lancelot and
Gareth are doing for the court of Arthur in the two preceding tales, and this is undoubtedly the reason that these
episodes about Tristram appear at this particular point in
the narrative. The contrast between the two courts which
is to be basic to Malory's political themes in the "Tristram"
begins in these first sections, and the chronological issue is
for the moment unimportant. We must remember that strict
chronology is important for Malory only when it has some
thematic relevance, as with the historical emergence of Arthurian society out of civil war and in the progressive decline of Arthurian society, both of which must be charted
along temporal lines, to make their point. For the moment
Malory is concerned with the quest for the ideal government,
and strict chronology has no thematic part to play. Consequently, Tales III, IV, and the first sections of V are placed
next to each other because their parallel episodes all depict
the way in which a society establishes the initial obligations
among its members to protect the community from external
threats.

II

We have seen how the thematic plan of Malory's book
is implicit in his structural innovations. His political designs

are equally apparent in his careful selection of literary models to suit the special needs of his political idealism. One of the most puzzling aspects of *Le Morte Darthur* is the diversity of narrative styles that it accommodates. Unlike the circumstance of the earlier versions of the story, we cannot characterize the genre of this book with any one term: it is not strictly chronicle, or romance, or even a combination of the two. As with the question of structure, an analysis of the "genre" of Malory's book reveals that its properties are very closely related to its themes and do not follow any recognizable laws of literary composition. Properly speaking there is no "genre" to which we can assign the book. The function of the book as a literary recreation of an historical ideal of life affects its use of different genres to a significant degree. To begin with, the style of the narrative is partly responsible for the fact that people read it in a superficial manner. The endless chronicling of battles with the tedious lists of names and deeds seems to carry very little thematic weight. Nevertheless, this style works very well to detract from the "romance" atmosphere of the story, while at the same time it lends a degree of historicity. By this use of the chronicler's style Malory gives his fiction the historical authority necessary to the establishment of a respectable ideal. On the other hand, he keeps a check on the chronicle material by allowing many of the conventions of the romance to undercut it, and thereby prevents the book from posing as history or pseudo-history. By not pretending to write a "factual history," he leaves himself room to fashion the characteristics of the Arthurian ideal as he views it. In examining Malory's use of different genres, then, we should not be surprised to discover that the peculiar mixture of kinds has a decidedly political cast.

The best general statement one can make about Malory's use of various literary types is that he has picked and chosen those elements from Arthurian chronicle and Arthurian romance which emphasize the social cohesiveness of the story. In other words, even though the *theme* of *Le Morte Darthur* exposes Arthurian society as basically self-destructive and even anarchical, the *form* of the book allows us to see the social structure behind the myth more clearly than we can in the earlier French and English treatments. What Malory avoids by his choice of different literary models for different aspects of his book is the propensity of the romances to ignore the social context of events. But at the same time he does not follow the tendency of chronicle to envelop one event (e.g., Arthur and his Round Table) in either the shroud of fortune, or in a cyclical vision of history, both of which would detract from its significance as a political tragedy. The effect of this combination of genres is that the story assumes an exemplary role as a political and social statement.

Perhaps Malory's peculiar use of genres can be illuminated by working out the definitions of chronicle and romance which apply to his various source materials, and then looking at what he has done with these models. Erich Auerbach has defined romance according to the degree and kind of reality which the genre admits.[6] Since it is on this issue of "realism" that Malory's book departs from the literary characteristics of his sources, Auerbach's essay is a good starting point. What characterizes romance atmosphere, as Auerbach understands it, is its total lack of sociological and economic foundations for the events in the narrative. The quest of the knight errant, unlike that in the *chanson de geste*, does not take place in a political framework and furthermore "serves no political function; it serves no practical reality at all; it has become absolute. It no longer has any purpose but that of self-realization."[7] From this statement we see that the chivalric ideal is principally an ideal of *personal* perfection. It it not primarily a social ideal.

Auerbach's definition of romance ought to be modified or clarified to this extent: to characterize medieval romance as lacking in a certain kind of realism is not the same thing as saying that we are dealing here with "escape" literature.

6. Erich Auerbach, *Mimesis* (New York, 1957), pp. 107–24.
7. *Ibid.*, pp. 116–17.

If his comments are taken together with the following admonition from Miss Tuve we have an adequate understanding of the genre of Malory's sources: "To be sure, romances were a genre that portrayed life idealistically, but on the assumption that it was a realistic portrayal of life. Setting a romance over against real life is a late habit, and we run the risk of confusing an opposition that is irrelevant here—the opposition between idealistic and *un*visionary—with a different distinction, between the fictive imaginary world and the world of daily life."[8]

Malory's major departure from the genre of his French sources is in the nature of his ideal. Unlike the narrative of the Vulgate Cycle, Malory's narrative gives events a political context, and his ideal is one of social fulfillment through personal perfection. What Vinaver has characterized somewhat disparagingly as Malory's "practical realism" is in fact not a vulgarization of the romance, but a shift away from the type of purely personal ideal which it portrays.[9] Similarly, since the story functions as an historical ideal of life, there is substantially more "authoritative" material like that found in the chronicles to give the narrative moral weight. No doubt Vinaver is often correct in pointing to the heavy-handedness of Malory's book by comparison with his sources; but what Vinaver does not appreciate is that Malory's reworking of the genres allows his story to encompass political and social realities not open to either romance or chronicle.

After sketching the general nature of Malory's departure from romance conventions, it is possible to outline his literary relationship to the conventions of chronicle and history. I include in this category Geoffrey, any chronicles Malory may have known, and other works such as those of Wace and Layamon which pose as historical records of actual events. Malory's exact knowledge of these sources remains undetermined. Nevertheless his inclusion of material and methods similar to those found in medieval chronicle and history is

8. Tuve, *Allegorical Imagery*, p. 342.
9. Vinaver, *Works of Malory*, I, 54.

easily discerned and has often been noted. The most obvious
of these characteristics are his insistence on the time of each
major segment of the narrative, the concern with causal relationships, the maintenance of historical distance from the
story (designated most frequently by the phrase "in tho
dayes"), and the immense amount of unwieldy chronicling
of personages and deeds. It should be obvious that the lack of
a political context and a sense of historical reality in the
romance is amply remedied by both chronicle and history.
Although in the Middle Ages these two forms differed greatly
in their attitudes towards the nature and importance of
"fact," they both supplied aspects of realism for Malory's
book unavailable in the literature of romance, which is specifically attuned to an examination of man in an ahistorical
context.

While there is no evidence that Malory read Geoffrey of
Monmouth, his affinity with Geoffrey's Arthurian historiography is striking and of immense significance. In a study
of English historiography, Robert W. Hanning illuminates
the special character of Geoffrey's *Historia* which sets it
apart from its predecessors in English historical writing.[10]
Hanning sees the Arthurian section of the *Historia Regum
Britanniae* as the transforming agent in Geoffrey's view of
history. His analysis of Geoffrey's book reveals a political
bias in the Arthurian sections which looks very much like
what I have described at the end of Chapter 2 as the political
character of Malory's Arthuriad. If Hanning's assessment
of the *Historia* is accurate, then the initial assumption (stated
in Chapter 2) that certain political motifs were already built
into the Arthurian story before it reached Malory receives
further confirmation. It seems to have taken a man of Malory's time to revive these motifs and recognize their affinity
with the general political concerns of his day. True enough,
the alliterative *Morte Arthure* is sufficient to account for the
heroic scale of this part of Malory's story and its nationalistic

10. Robert W. Hanning, *The Vision of History in Early Britain*
(New York, 1966), pp. 139ff.

overtones, but there is an overlay of political sophistication in Malory's version which points to another source—either Geoffrey or someone like him.

I shall summarize Hanning's analysis of the *Historia*, and show that both Malory's affinities with Geoffrey and his departures from the latter's interpretation of historical events are conditioned by the political issues outlined in the preceding chapter. Hanning sets Geoffrey apart from the works of his predecessors on the basis of the role which Geoffrey allows personal fortune to play in national affairs: "In the *Historia*, the regulation of history by repetitive patterns of personal behavior and national progress has replaced the Christian system of movement toward a final happiness or reward."[11] It is the absence of the idea of eschatological fulfillment in Geoffrey's history which allows its creator to emphasize the individual as a moving force in history:

> In many cases where tension exists in the *Historia Regum Brittaniae* between personal needs or desires and national stability, the crux of the situation is a special relationship of some kind, i.e., between two brothers, or cousins, or even between father and daughter. . . . A common development underlies and relates all these fabricated crises: the individual begins to emerge as a person from the pattern of history, *a person moreover whose extra-political relationships, especially kindred ones, determine his actions, even if the result is national chaos.*[12]

Here we can see that special connection between private and public issues which is at the center of fifteenth-century political theory and consequently of Malory's interpretation of the Arthurian story. Like Geoffrey, Malory is impressed by the connection between the personal fortunes and needs of the individual and the fate of the nation. The entire import of the Arthurian story for Geoffrey lay in the fact that in this instance the connection between king and kingdom is closer and more crucial in its consequences than at any other time in the history of Britain. Geoffrey's gift to the Arthurian

11. *Ibid.*, p. 171.
12. *Ibid.*, p. 143. (Italics mine.)

tradition is the tragic sense he evokes by emphasizing this contrast between British fortunes at the time of Arthur and the total collapse which followed his defeat: "One moment, it seems, Arthur is alive and Britain rules the world; the next the king is dead and the nation divided."[13]

Malory takes up where Geoffrey's interpretation of history leaves off. That is, the Arthurian tragedy as Geoffrey presents it is transformed by Malory into an object lesson on the necessity of *continuous* political forms. The tragedy of the Arthurian story is not simply the death of Arthur, but more significantly the fact that here is a society which has not provided itself with the structure for accommodating the death of one individual. It has no eternal public sphere which will survive personal catastrophes. As Hanning points out, Arthur's death in the *Historia* is presented as a domestic crisis which permanently cripples the nation.[14] Although the nation can make partial recoveries in certain areas, a full scale recovery of the Arthurian political structure is not possible. The forcefulness of Geoffrey's presentation of the tragedy may have left its mark on Malory's interpretation of the story as a warning that public and private spheres in government must be kept separate.

On this latter issue of the story as a moral lesson Malory differs from Geoffrey's interpretation. There is no sense in the *Historia* that Arthurian society is in any way responsible for its own end. Geoffrey's emphases are first on the effect of personal interests on national interests, and secondly on the tyranny of fortune over both. "Arthur's reign provides the prime instance of Geoffrey's dual historical vision. His reign illustrates the pinnacle of human greatness and at the same time serves as the mighty *exemplum* of Fortune's thrusting greatness down to sudden destruction."[15] Malory rejects the role of fortune as executrix of the final catastrophe. He even omits the climatic "Fortune-passage" from the alliter-

13. *Ibid.*, p. 148.
14. *Ibid.*
15. *Ibid.*, p. 139.

ative *Morte*, his source for Tale II. His political bias led him instead to examine the *structure* of Arthurian society, and he found the seeds of its downfall there. But the impact of the Arthurian story as an example of the connection between the personal and the public spheres is the real debt which *Le Morte Darthur* owes either directly or indirectly to the *Historia Regum Britanniae*.

As we have seen in the structural analysis of the Balin story, Malory had a very good understanding of the way in which extra-political relationships bear on national welfare. His interest in the problem is akin to Fortescue's concern with the threats of the *persona volunta* to the *persona publica*. Geoffrey's impact on the Arthurian story was to highlight this problem in an historical context. Malory's addition to the theme is to analyze the story with the same terms which his contemporaries would have used to judge it: how successfully does this political structure mediate between private interests and public welfare? Malory's difference from Geoffrey is clear here. Geoffrey does not judge. The historian who sees history as the victim of fortune can not pass judgment on the actions of her victims. Furthermore, as Merlin's prophecies in the *Historia* indicate (*Historia*, VII, 4), Geoffrey holds a decidedly apocalyptic view of the universe in which everything, including history, is doomed to come to an abrupt stop. By contrast, Malory is very much a man of his century and does not hold an apocalyptic view of things; for him historical events have consequences in a foreseeable future. Political forms must therefore be judged with a view to their continuity.

Quite naturally, then, Malory accepted the idealization of Arthurian society characteristic of romance while at the same time he satisfied the impulse of the chronicler and historian to provide an historical and political context for this ideal. By combining these characteristics of two separate genres, Malory provided the Arthurian story with all of the requirements of an historical ideal of life.

This discussion of Malory's use of different genres to en-

compass his political themes ought to conclude with some
consideration of his audience, since the function of this combination of chronicle, history, and romance is only clear in
the context of his readers. Auerbach in *Mimesis* and in *Literary Language and its Public in the Later Middle Ages*
stresses the point that in the later Middle Ages the aristocracy had been robbed of the practical functions associated
with feudalism.[16] As a consequence of this functional crisis
the aristocracy formed a literary public which "proceeded
to describe its own life in extrahistorical terms as an absolute aesthetic configuration without practical purpose."[17]
Auerbach is describing romance as the ideal which the aristocracy clung to in order to disguise its own absence of function. Considered in this light, Malory's contribution to literary history is unique. His combination of the idealization
of romance with the political issues of his day satisfies two
needs at once: it gives the "functionless" class its accustomed
entertainment, and at the same time reassures it that it can
have a function. In his asides as narrator Malory most often
acts as a moral guide who shows the reader the virtues and
dangers of the society he describes and thus imparts to his
audience the knowledge necessary for their proper partic-
ipation in political matters.

What Malory has done in re-creating the Arthurian ideal
along political lines is to follow a popular trend in medieval
English literature which Auerbach defines and dates as beginning in the fourteenth century. Scholars have usually
confined Malory's literary inheritance to the specifically Arthurian material of England and France. But Auerbach's
brief comments on the popular non-Arthurian literature of
the fourteenth century make this material seem crucial to the
moral background of *Le Morte Darthur*: "The popular and
indigenous character of English literature of the fourteenth
century is reflected in a practical sense of what is right in

16. Erich Auerbach, *Literary Language and Its Public in Late Latin
Antiquity and in the Middle Ages* (New York, 1965), p. 333.
17. Auerbach, *Mimesis*, p. 120.

men's dealings with each other. As in other countries, this ethical sense had developed on the basis of the medieval *exempla*, but more than elsewhere it was oriented towards political activity. The moralistic satire of the time had at its core an instinct for what was socially desirable.''[18] I know of no effort to relate Malory to this particular body of earlier literature, and yet its ethical themes and political concerns seem central to Malory's morality, as the following thematic analysis of his book will show.

Once the general characteristics of genre and structure are set forth with their political implications, it becomes easier to follow the unfolding of the historical ideal in Malory's narrative. The last chapter of this study is reserved for the material which indicates Malory's ultimate dissatisfaction with chivalry as an historical and political ideal. The remainder of this chapter is devoted to pinpointing the political issues outlined in Chapter 2 as they appear in *Le Morte Darthur*.

III

Tale I

In discussing the source of Tale I Vinaver praises the narrative art of the *Suite du Merlin* because its use of *entrelacement* allows for the introduction of an infinite number of themes. He also points out that as a consequence of this method, the work can never really be complete; there is no end towards which this kind of narrative can move.[19] In Malory's "Tale of King Arthur," the narrative method of the *Suite* is reversed. *Entrelacement* is omitted, and the tale allowed to come to a stop, because as a unit it is wholly devoted to one purpose—establishing the Arthurian ideal and displaying the political foundations of Arthurian society.

Malory omits the first thirty-eight leaves of the French version, which included Uther's founding of the Round

18. Auerbach, *Literary Language*, p. 326.
19. Vinaver, *Works of Malory*, III, 1265–73.

Table and other events before the birth of Arthur. His
narrative focuses on Arthur, and in fifteenth-century fashion
he begins by structuring the story in terms of the king's relation to the polity and of the definition of that polity. The
additions and changes in the first tale accentuate the sharp
break in time between the chaotic England of Uther and the
promise of stability and unity under the leadership of Arthur and his Round Table. Malory robs Uther of the honor
accorded him in the *Suite* where he is the founder of the
Round Table, because in *Le Morte Darthur* the Round Table
must be Arthur's creation and central concern.

The conditions of Arthur's election also bear the earmarks
of a fifteenth-century kingship. Malory goes to great lengths
to establish the authenticity of Arthur's claim to the throne.
It is characteristic of the French romances, and also thematically necessary to them, that Arthur's merits and rights
be shrouded in mystery. He has in these romances no very
clear virtues which predispose him to rule. This mystery is
part of the romance tradition, as Rosemond Tuve shows:
"The mystery of Arthur's supernatural election and the
question of his fitness as chief of such a fellowship is felt
even in the prose romances."[20] But because Malory is dealing with the issue of kingship and with a societal ideal, he
prefers to do without mystery and to present a king with
clearly defined fifteenth-century qualifications.

Numerous instances in the Merlin section of Tale I illustrate this tendency. The French romance is content to have
Merlin prophesy that Arthur will be king. Malory, however, has inserted a passage in which Uther gives his blessing
to Arthur in front of the assembled nobles (7). Similarly,
the implications of the sword in the stone are somewhat different in Malory's version. Malory's version says that who-
ever accomplishes the feat will be "RIGHTWYS KYNGE BORNE
OF ALL ENGLOND" (7). Here he emphasizes the importance
of Arthur's birthright and of his *unification* of the kingdom.
One further instance of Malory's concern for Arthur's tes-

20. Tuve, *Allegorical Imagery*, p. 351.

timony is the final test at the feast of the Pentecost where Arthur pulls out the sword before the lords and commons. In a sourceless passage the commons demand Arthur for their king and declare it is God's will. Also in numerous sourceless passages throughout Tale I members of the Arthurian community and outsiders as well comment on Arthur's virtues of bravery, devotion to the common good, and ability to lead.

That Malory has designed the Arthurian ideal along fifteenth-century lines is thus abundantly clear from the first section of Tale I. The ideal, as we should have expected, is devoted to the accomplishment of unity and thereby of peace. Immediately after Arthur's coronation an original passage occurs concerning Arthur's subjugation of the Northern rebellion and his stabilization of the realm: "But within fewe yeres after Arthur wan alle the North, Scotland and alle that were under their obeissaunce, also Walys; a parte of it helde ayenst Arthur, but he overcam hem al as he dyd the remenaunt thurgh the noble prowesse of hymself and his knyghtes of the Round Table (11)." Vinaver says that Malory's mention of Arthur and his Round Table here shows ignorance of the rest of his source, but Malory is not really speaking prematurely; he is describing what the Round Table was to do in the future, not at the moment of the coronation when it did not exist.[21] This method is quite in keeping with Merlin's prophecy on the following page where he tells of Arthur's subjection of *all* Britain. This sourceless passage and others like it demonstrate the connection between the metaphor of unity contained in the king's body politic and the actual accomplishments of such a political body in the achievements of Arthur and his Round Table.

Many other passages in the Merlin section indicate that the theory of kingship of which Merlin is the executor is being designed with contemporary issues in mind. On several occasions (e.g., 13 and 28–29) Malory adds passages where Merlin gives advice to Arthur on how to behave as a king, and specifically how he should reward his men. Ban and

21. Vinaver, *Works of Malory*, III, 1285.

Bors also indirectly advise Arthur (27) that a king's worship is increased according to the quality of the men he can attract to him. These passages display a contemporary concern for the king in his public capacity which does not appear in the French texts.

I have noted above that the major events in Arthur's career leading up to his election occur on days which in the Church calendar mark significant and parallel events in both the life of Christ and the founding of the Church. There are in Malory, moreover, direct comments which underline this parallel. When he summons the barons on Christmas day Merlin makes a parallel between the "Kyng of mankynde" and the King of England (7). These parallels and references in Malory's narrative seem to bring out the double nature of Arthur's kingship and relate it directly to the theory of the king's twinned being. At the opening of the "Torre and Pellinor" section of Tale I we are told: "In the begynnyng of Arthure aftir he was chosyn kynge by *adventure* and by *grace*. . ." (71, italics mine). This again is original with Malory. Malory seems to insist upon the christological associations of Arthur's rule for the same reason that political theorists from John of Salisbury to Fortescue used such associations to establish the sacred nature of the state, the King's peace, and the King's justice. These are the things touching kingship, and they are therefore inviolable and necessary to the perpetuation of the realm.

Perhaps the most telling piece of evidence which attests Malory's contemporary political bias in the first section of Tale I is the coronation of Arthur. In the *Suite*, Arthur's first sworn obligation is to the Church, whereas in Malory the king promises to stand with true justice and to right grievances occurring before his reign. Vinaver comments that these conditions of coronation are totally out of keeping with the French Arthurian tradition. What Malory has actually done is to bring this episode into line with the much discussed English coronation oath and to stress the point that the crown is public property and at the service of public utility. Arthur's first act is to place himself at the disposal of his people. His kingship obviously exists on a contractual basis. Furthermore, the king promises to the lords and commons to be a true king, which in Malory means that he will "stand with true justyce fro thens forth the dayes of this lyf" (11). The emphasis on justice as the first and most important obligation of the king is another echo of contemporary political thought. Fortescue, recalling the coronation oath, described justice as the primary obligation of the crown and the sole means of its perpetuation.

The political slant of the Balin story has already been discussed as an example of the thematic dimension of Malory's structural technique. The Merlin section has established the conditions of Arthur's kingship, and in the Balin section Malory sets forth the problem which measures the success of a government: that of mediating between private needs and the public interest. The Balin story, Malory's handling of Arthur's coronation, and his time sequence are the most striking departures from the *Suite* thus far in the narrative. In all three instances we can see that his alterations have the effect of shaping the story as an historical ideal of life and demonstrating its political relevance to his own time.

The problem in the Balin story is ultimately that of unity and world peace; these are the things which Balin jeopardizes as a result of the Dolorous Stroke. As Vinaver has rightly noted, in the *Suite* Balin is "a victim of relentless destiny which is neither a just retribution for a misdeed nor a simple accident, but part of a tragic pattern of human existence."[22] But Malory has changed the emphasis of the story: he eliminates the role of fate and replaces it with the dynamic conflict of individual and community.

That the Balin story is to function as a moral vignette for Arthurian society is amply clear from the framing device Malory constructs for it. The opening establishes the story as occurring pre-Round Table at a time of disunity and civil war. The story ends with a sourceless passage describing

22. Vinaver, *Works of Malory*, III, 1275.

Merlin's return to Arthur to report the sad tale of Balin's end. This latter episode and others like it where Malory adds an eye witness report to the king seem designed to be the author's admonition concerning the dangers that inhere in any society; these are the dangers which the Round Table will have to be strong enough to circumvent. Furthermore, the actual events in the story involve a kind of disruption and fatality which the French version only hints at. Unlike the situation in the source, the prophecy that Balin will kill his brother if he keeps the sword is fulfilled, and reiterated in the *explicit* to the section. The theme of fratricide and blood feud is thereby underlined as a prefiguration of later events.

Significantly enough, "The Knight with the Two Swords," which contains the foreboding pre-history of Arthur's court, is followed immediately by the "Torre and Pellinor" section in which Malory sets up the fellowship of knights to function as a political corrective for the problems which threaten the realm. Malory's development of the Arthurian fellowship, which begins here, is by far the most consistently original feature of his book. He stretches the political aspects of the Round Table as far as possible in the direction of contemporary corporational thinking. But at the same time that he presents Arthurian society as potentially ideal, he also exposes its limitations as a governing body, lets these two currents run simultaneously for a while, and then when the exigencies of plot demand it, fully exposes the weaknesses of the Arthurian code as a means of government.

The "Torre and Pellinor" section begins with Arthur's wedding and the founding of the Round Table. It concludes with Malory's version of the Arthurian code which binds the members to each other and to the king. We can see very clearly here that Malory is working the Round Table into a parallel with the physiological metaphor of the body politic. The central portion of the section is devoted to the quests of Torre, Pellinore, and Gawain, the newly made knights. The admonitions in the code at the end of the story have their sources in the adventures of these knights. As extensions of the king's justice, the limbs of the political body of which Arthur is the head, they are the agents of equity and mercy. Like the prince in John of Salisbury, Bracton, and Fortescue, Arthur is not the active arbiter of justice; his government is a corporational one, and its members perform the king's justice. On two significant occasions Malory has included original comments on the meaning of these quests in the context of governing the realm. The issue of all the episodes is that of mercy, and Gaheris's rebuke of Gawain is the first of these explanations of how mercy is to be employed:

"Alas," seyde Gaherys, "that ys fowle and shamefully done, for that shame shall never frome you. Also ye sholde gyff mercy unto them that aske mercy, for a knyght withoute mercy ys withoute worship." (79).

"Thou new made knyght, thou haste shamed thy knyghthode, for a knyght withoute mercy ys dishonoured. Also thou haste slayne a fayre lady to thy grete shame unto the worldys ende, and doute the nat thou shalt have grete nede of mercy or thou departe frome us." (80).

There is of course a direct echo of these original statements in the Arthurian code which Malory inserts at the end of the section: "gyff mercy unto hym that askith mercy, uppon payne of forfiture [of their] worship and lordship of kynge Arthure for evirmore" (91).

Aside from delineating the function of Arthur and the Round Table as head and limbs of the body politic, the "Torre and Pellinor" section focuses on one other related and crucial issue in medieval English political thought. From the time of Bracton when the king began to appear as an administrator of a public sphere rather than as a personal liege lord, the choice of a council, or limbs of the body politic, was of crucial importance. The strength of the state depended on the king's ability to attract the best councilors. In a similar vein, the founding of the Round Table in the "Torre and Pellinor" section and its expansion in books III, IV, and V when new members are brought in reveals

Malory's concern with this problem: "For by the noble felyshyp of the Rounde Table was kynge Arthur upborne, and
by their nobeles the Kynge and all the realme was ever in
quyet and reste" (850). Malory's addition here underlines
his concern with the contemporary interest in achieving unity
and stability by means of a corporational structure.

The code itself, the culmination of these quests, displays
a striking concern for the welfare of the realm. The French
text concentrates solely on the spiritual relationship between the knights, and the king in the *Suite* is only *primus
inter pares*. Malory undermines these religious overtones of
his source in favor of utilizing the Round Table as a political
rather than as a spiritual body. The oath which the knights
swear to at each feast of the Pentecost is basically a code
of public service. At its center are the spiritual virtues of
mercy and justice to be sure, but the context of these virtues
has been changed. The code is specifically directed at eliminating the tyranny of one individual over another, at pro-
tecting the weak from the strong, and at ensuring them of
"hir ryghtes." The acts of the king's political body, his
members of the Round Table, are not acts of private individuals; they are done for the community which the king's body
politic represents. Arthur's code makes this fact amply clear
to his followers. The divine attributes of justice and mercy
are recast from the French where they safeguard the spiritual
welfare of the Round Table. In this code they are more
narrowly defined as instruments for governing the society
outside the fellowship.

In the last three sections of Tale I, Malory's alterations
in his French source serve three principal functions directly
connected with his political themes: first, they work toward
establishing Arthur as a king of sufficient stature to fulfill
the requirements which a fifteenth-century jurist like Fortescue would set forth; secondly, they expand the external
threats to unity and peace to show the effectiveness with
which the Round Table deals with them; finally, they sharpen
the thematic content of several episodes to make them dem-

onstrate the governmental ideal of justice and mercy. The groundwork of the political ideal is laid down here and is elaborated upon in Tales II, III, and IV.

In the opening of "The War With the Five Kings" Malory has added a passage in which Arthur declares his personal devotion to his country. " 'Alas!' seyde Arthure, 'yet had I never reste one monethe syne I was kyng crowned of this londe. Now shall I never reste tylle I mete with tho kyngis in a fayre felde, that I make myne avow; for my trwe lyege peple shall not be destroyed in my defaughte. Therefore go with me who so woll, and abyde who that wyll.' " (93). On the following page there is a second insertion where the five kings discuss Arthur's ability to attract the "floure of chevalry of the worlde" to fight on his side, and his personal courage in the face of great odds. These and similar passages mentioned earlier (e.g., 43) bring out that aspect of fifteenth-century political theory which places the king's personal safety at the service of the state. In Tale II we can see how Malory took a different source and used it to adumbrate this theme of *pro patria mori*.

The effect of these kinds of additions is to create an atmosphere of reverence around the king which will render instances of disloyalty all the more abominable. The events of the next section of Tale I, "Arthur and Accolon," are colored in just this way. In the *Suite*, the corresponding episode rests heavily on the use of supernatural effects. Vinaver assumes that Malory here and elsewhere was simply uncomfortable with the aspects of the marvelous which he found in his sources and that he therefore omitted them. Often Vinaver accuses him of misunderstanding the use of magic in the French, and thus bungling the theme. Inadvertently, however, Vinaver has hit upon a very telling point in his analysis of Malory's "Arthur and Accolon": "In the story of Arthur's fight with Accolon what impresses Malory is not the part played by the enchanted sword and its scabbard . . . but the seemingly *monstrous fact that Accolon is fighting against his anointed lord*; to make this humanly credible he blackens Accolon's character and uses the story as an example of criminal behavior, and not of the power of witchcraft."[23] There is no suggestion of treason in the French, but in Malory it is mentioned on three occasions (104, 107, 110). Vinaver is quite right in recognizing the tone of moral outrage in these passages. The emphasis on Accolon's sin against his anointed lord brings us back to the fifteenth-century reverence for the sacred and spiritual body of the king.

The treasonous plot on Arthur's life also becomes an occasion for another piece of Malory's political moralizing. The episode is resolved by what appears a model of kingly behavior. In a lengthy passage (107) Arthur grants mercy to Accolon and displays that innate feeling for justice which John of Salisbury and Fortescue describe as belonging to the true king. Besides granting Accolon mercy Arthur arrives at an equitable solution for the case of Damas and his brother, Outlake. In the French Damas and Outlake have engaged in a straightforward dispute about land; there is no question of tyranny or cruelty involved. In Malory, Damas is characterized as being without mercy and guilty of that form of tyranny which one subject inflicts on another. This alteration in the story allows us to see Arthur restoring the justice of which he is guardian and living example (107–8).

These themes of treason, justice, and mercy continue to be important in the last section of Tale I, "Gawain, Ywain, and Marhalt." The episode of the Magic Mantle and the occasion of Ywain's exile are separate in Malory's source. Malory has brought in Morgan's plot at this point because he is still working out the themes of treason and trust in his narrative. In the Accolon section Arthur has already said that he has trusted Morgan more than his wife and all his kin. But by this time he has learned not to misplace his trust, and therefore he forces the damsel to wear the poisoned mantle first. The other major episode of this section, Pelleas and Ettard, also involves the limits of trust in the stable

23. Vinaver, *Works of Malory*, III, 1277. (Italics mine.)

community. Malory discards the courtly love theme and makes the story reflect the problem of trust *between* members of the society. Pelleas's appeal to Gawain (122) to repay his trust and not to betray him with Ettard is Malory's addition, as is Gawain's reply in which he promises to do his "trew parte" (123).

I have shown in such detail Malory's changes in each section of Tale I because the idealization of Arthur and the Round Table which appears in the next three tales begins here. It is not surprising then that the first indications of the weaknesses of the ideal appear at the end of Tale II. These hints are appropriately placed in this position because their significance becomes apparent only in Tale V, which follows Tale II chronologically.

We have seen how Malory has altered the *Suite* to include political themes absent in his source. He has abandoned the kind of mysterious kingship accorded Arthur in the French romances where the sovereign's position is simply a given and not a question of merit. He also eliminates the role of fortune in the fate of the Round Table in favor of direct ascription of cause and effect to important events. In making these changes, Malory has either intentionally or unintentionally brought Arthur and the Round Table into line with the corporational thinking of his time, so that at least initially Arthurian society seems the type of perfect government which John of Salisbury had thought possible only for man in a state of innocence.

As it is represented in Tales I, II, III, and IV, Arthurian society is the fulfillment of Fortescue's ideal of mixed political rule. The ideal remains intact, however, because it is defined only by the external elements which it combats. Its character at this point is determined by the action of the narrative: that is, just as Arthurian order is imposed upon the world by subduing elements hostile to it, so the Round Table is shaped by its opposition to *external* threats. In their analyses of Tale I, Wright and Moorman see the treacherous activities of Morgan le Fay as symptomatic of a lack of trust within the Arthurian community itself.[24] But this reading errs by anticipating the events of the last tales and interpreting the first tale in their light.[25] In Malory's version, the Round Table is established because treachery and disorder exist; these elements are not yet products of its own weaknesses.

That Malory intended this development from external to internal crisis seems likely from the addition and order of two prophecies he places in the first book of Tale I. In the Merlin story he omits a prophecy of the Grail quest which appears in the French and includes instead two other forecasts: the first foretells the successful establishment of Arthur's kingdom through conquest (12); the second indicates both the nobility of his fellowship and at the same time forecasts its destruction from *within* (41). The order and content of these prophecies exactly duplicate the thematic development of the ideal of fellowship. The tension and sense of crisis are therefore present from the beginning. Malory deliberately focuses our attention on *how* the fellowship will fail because he is ultimately concerned with the bases of human government. The suspense of the book is sustained by the moral paradox of Arthurian society's great successes and the gradual unfolding of its political instability.

Tale II

Turning next to the political themes of Tale II is somewhat confusing since chronologically it seems to belong after Tales III and IV. By keeping this fact in mind we can account for those premonitions of internal strife which appear towards the end of the tale. To begin with, however, Tale II is primarily an elaboration of two of the main political themes which reinforce the Arthurian ideal. First, there is the theme of England's governmental mission as successor

24. Charles Moorman, *The Book of Kyng Arthur: The Unity of Malory's "Morte Darthur"* (Lexington, 1965), p. 85.

25. T. L. Wright, "The Tale of King Arthur," *Malory's Originality*, ed. R. M. Lumiansky (Baltimore, 1964), pp. 60–61.

to Israel and Rome which I mentioned in Chapter 2. Malory underlines the significance of the Roman campaign by actually having Arthur crowned emperor. There is no hint of such an event in the French sources, although in the alliterative *Morte Arthure*—Malory's source for Tale II—a cunning cardinal tells Arthur that the pope shall crown him emperor (1. 3183). That Malory actually invents the episode of the coronation is evidence of his interest in Arthurian England as the "new Rome." The ideal of the new Rome is not simply a highly inventive form of chauvinism; it is an indication of the seriousness with which the "ideal" form of government was regarded.

The other aspect of the Arthurian ideal central to Malory's "Tale of Arthur and the Emperor Lucius" is the notion of the king's supreme devotion to the country and to the political body of which he is the head. Arthur's behavior here and in certain original passages already noted in Tale I is exemplary of the ideal of *pro patria mori*. Throughout the Middle Ages the parallel between Christ and king was applied to the king's activities in various ways. In matters of war, for instance, one often encounters the notion that the king's sacrifice of personal safety and indeed of his life itself was not only appropriate to his office but expected of him.[26] The christological parallel is obvious. The fact that certain jurists in the fourteenth and fifteenth centuries argued against the expense and dangers of such *caritas*, demonstrates that in Malory's time it was still a live issue, although the influence of those who would so lightly dispense with their king's personal welfare was undoubtedly waning.[27]

In Malory's second tale we find that he has taken good advantage of the materials built into his source, the alliterative *Morte Arthure*, and enlarged on them to magnify Arthur's devotion to the body politic and the common good as well. The significance of Arthur's combat with the giant

26. Ernst Kantorowicz, *The King's Two Bodies: A Study in Mediaeval Political Theology* (Princeton, 1957), pp. 232–72.
27. *Ibid.*, pp. 256ff.

is well defined in the poem. Arthur, as the philosopher says,
is to purge the land of a tyrannical monster by doing "batayle
by thyself alone" (143). In Malory, moreover, he does battle
as the dragon which he saw in his dream, and in so doing
saves all the kingdoms he has conquered (symbolized in the
dream by the dragon's wings), as well as the knights of the
Round Table (represented in the dream by the dragon's tail).

The portrayal of Arthur's sacrifice of personal safety for
the common good was certainly one of the attractions which
the alliterative poem held for Malory. In addition to the
combat with the giant, Arthur also appears in numerous
places as a king whose ultimate concern is for his knights and
co-governors of his realm. Malory expands this theme in a
number of original passages: in a speech by Idres (151);
in Arthur's address to the wounded Gawain (152); in his
distress over the needless casualties when his men are over-
matched (157); and finally in his heroic rescue of his fellows (161). These passages, undoubtedly Malory's additions,
indicate the degree of his idealization of Arthurian society in
fifteenth-century political terms. They suggest, as does the
fight with the giant, that Arthur functions here as both the
role model and a savior for his followers.

There are still other instances of Malory's tendency to
make Arthurian society supply political ideals for his dis-
illusioned time. His source contained general elements which
were highly congenial to his purpose, such as Arthur's mag-
nificent stature in the eyes of foreigners (1. 136), and his
responsible attitude in matters of policy, where he refers to
the judgment of his council (1. 144). To this material Malory
adds specific details concerning Arthur as the distributor of
justice throughout conquered lands: "There was none that
playned on his parte, ryche nothir poore" (175). When he
establishes Lancelot and Bors as the governors of the cap-
tured lands Arthur instructs them in their behavior as rulers:
"Cause youre lyege men to know you as for their kynde
lorde, and *suffir never your soveraynté to be alledged with your
subjects, nother the soveraygne of your persone and londys*"

(176). (Italics mine.) This statement on the double sovereignty of person and office, or of public and private persons, is just what we could expect from a fifteenth-century work advising a prince about how to manage his roles.

The Roman victory is Arthur's, not that of fortune, and it is a victory born first of self-sacrifice and secondly of an ability to command a quasi-religious devotion from his men. England has literally and figuratively become the successor to Rome. The rebellion of Mordred which follows in the source has no place in this kind of narrative because, as Malory sees it, rebellion is a direct outgrowth of the king's governmental disability. In Malory the king himself creates the occasion for the final catastrophe. In the alliterative *Morte*, the king is victimized by fortune, and Mordred's rebellion does not arise from a collapse of the Arthurian political structure, but from the turning of fortune's wheel. When we see signs of political instability in *Le Morte Darthur*, they have internal sources. The author of the alliterative poem is making a point about human destiny and fortitude while Malory's version of the story plays upon the question of man's social responsibility and the stability of his institutions.[28] After Arthur rescues some of his knights Malory as commentator introduces the theme of envy and rivalry within the fellowship, which will develop largely unnoticed by the members of the Round Table throughout the next tales: "for oftetymes thorow envy grete hardynesse is shewed that hath bene the deth of many kyd knyghtes; for thoughe they speke fayre many one unto other, yet whan they be in batayle eyther wolde beste be praysed" (161).

Here we catch the briefest glimpse of the narrator's point of view. Chivalry, the *modus vivendi* of this highly ideal political structure, contains at its heart a self-destructive and an anti-social tendency: the necessity of winning worship

28. See *Morte Arthure,* ed. Edmond Brock, *Early English Text Society,* O.S. 8 (1871), 1. 3183, and R. M. Lumiansky, "The Alliterative *Morte Arthure*: The Concept of Medieval Tragedy and the Cardinal Virtue of Fortitude," *Medieval and Renaissance Studies,* III (1968), 95–118.

for the king often forces one to do so at the expense of one's
fellows, at the risk of envy, and at the cost of eliciting revenge. All three consequences place the order and stability
of the realm in peril. It is dramatically significant at this
point that while Arthur's actions in this tale work against
the envy inherent in the chivalric code, he himself as king
offers no explicit code of conduct to combat envy until his
speech at the end of "The Great Tournament" in Tale VII.

Thus far the evidence of Malory's fashioning the Arthurian
story as an historical ideal of life is overwhelming. Whatever
slight evidences there have been that this ideal cannot withstand the political demands a fifteenth-century thinker might
make on it, have no direct impact on the reader at this point.
Tales III and IV continue the thematic development of I,
and II; they too invest Arthurian society with the political
ideals of the fifteenth century. In both tales we can credit
Malory with the structure and a substantial part of the content of the narrative. Whether or not Malory has consciously
designed his material so that it works in this way cannot of
course be determined. What I have done thus far is to show
the emergence of contemporary issues by analyzing Malory's
additions and structural arrangements. In the next two
tales the themes emerge directly out of Malory's alterations
of his source; that is, as in the first two tales, the alterations
become the most significant indicators of Malory's thematic
direction and "coincidentally" display a great concern with
contemporary political issues. The matter of intention is
best left alone. The evidence of these first four tales allows
us to say convincingly that Malory displays the Arthurian
story as a political model which appears to fulfill the contemporary demands for continuity and unity of governmental forms.

Tales III and IV

"The Tale of Lancelot" bears the structure of the
quest. Malory has arranged his story so that the material
which intervenes in the French source between the first two

episodes does not break up the thematic development in his version. Lancelot's quest concerns the true nature of chivalry and justice, and he is countered in each episode by threats of treachery or treason. Malory has brought the first two episodes of the tale together to focus on the quester's fight with treasonous forces. In these episodes, as in the rest of the tale, Arthur's fellowship in the person of Lancelot truly acts as the extended self of the king. Each accomplishment concludes with Lancelot's sending the conquered knight to Arthur's court to do homage to the queen. In this way the unity of the kingdom is assured.

Vinaver, who rarely attributes any thematic value to Malory's alterations, points out that "The Tale of Lancelot" departs from the romance tradition not only by omitting the large digression between the first two episodes, but also in the nature of its descriptive techniques. He notes that Malory's descriptions of fighting are infinitely more graphic than those of his source and comments that "he [Malory] had not yet discovered the distinction between the epic enjoyment of picturesque slaughter and the refined and abstract presentation of battle-scenes in romance."[29] If we are reading Malory with an eye on his thematic concerns, however, it is clear that the great amount of violence in any given episode is thematically significant. He has arranged the narrative in Tale III to make it portray the ideal political structure triumphing over those elements which would threaten peace and justice. The violence of the episodes is directly proportionate to the seriousness with which Malory regards these threats. The atmosphere of romance is purposely made to give way to a sense of the actuality of civil war. Again Malory's way of reading or handling his source allows contemporary concerns to break through the conventions of romance to invest them with a political reality.

The danger of all purely "political" interpretations of *Le Morte Darthur* is that they have a difficult time accounting for the role of the love story in the catastrophe. But read-

29. Vinaver, *Works of Malory,* III, 1402.

ing "The Tale of Lancelot" closely we discover that Malory
drops several hints that women are to be considered an additional threat to the stability of the realm. By keeping in mind
that Malory has chosen episodes for the tale in which women
are a motivating force in the action, it becomes easier to
understand, first, Lancelot's peculiar comments on women,
and secondly, the role of courtly love in the story as a whole.
When the damsel asks Lancelot why he favors no woman
except Guenevere he replies:

"I may nat warne peple to speke of me what hit pleasyth hem.
But for to be a weddyd man, I thynke hit nat, for than I muste
couche with hir and leve armys and turnaments, batellys and adventures. And as for to sey to take my pleasaunce with peramours,
that woll I refuse: in prencipall for drede of God, for knyghtes
that bene adventures sholde nat be advoutrers nothir lecherous, for
than they be nat happy nother fortunate unto the werrys; for
other they shall be overcom with a sympler knyght than they be
hemself, other ellys they shall sle by unhappe and hir cursednesse
bettir men than they be hemself. And so who that usyth peramours
shall be unhappy, and all thynge unhappy that is aboute them"
(194–95).

Accepting R. M. Lumiansky's plausible thesis that at this
stage the Lancelot-Guenevere adultery has not begun (and
this passage certainly supports such a reading), then we are
left with Malory's view that because women are involved
only with the private lives of men, they are potentially disruptive and destructive forces in the public sphere.[30] Lancelot's
words, despite their fatuous tone, certainly bring out this
point. Here as elsewhere Lancelot is behaving in a highly
idealized way. He has managed to concentrate wholly on
matters of public life, honor, and reputation. He has not
relegated women to the appropriate private sphere, but has
ruled them out of his life altogether. Such idealized behavior
obviously involves so significant a degree of deprivation that

30. R. M. Lumiansky, "The Relationship of Lancelot and Guenevere
in Malory's 'Tale of Lancelot.' " *Modern Language Notes*, LXVIII
(1953), 86–91.

it eventually undermines its own purpose. For the moment, however, the ideal seems unassailable.

If we take the role of women in Tale III and the moralizing which accompanies their presence, and apply it to the book as a whole the relationship between courtly love and Malory's political model is immediately apparent. Malory's peculiar "mishandling" of courtly love is a direct result of the fact that he treats all major man-woman relationships as matters of crucial *political* importance. The love stories no longer have a romantic life of their own, because as Malory sees them, they impinge on the public sphere and therefore present a governmental problem. This is not to say that Malory is without romantic sentiment; rather he has a very sharp tragic sense which recognizes the fatal consequences for the lovers of their encroachment upon the public sphere. In the last tales we discover that the matter of courtly love constitutes one of the major instances of the Round Table's failure to mediate between private and public spheres.

Tales III and IV are linked very closely together in structure and theme. Whether or not "The Tale of Gareth" is wholly Malory's composition is somewhat irrelevant in the light of its thematic function. If Malory did not write it, he certainly seized upon it as the perfect companion piece to Tale III in the establishment of the Arthurian ideal. "Gareth" begins with the feast of the Pentecost, "Lancelot" ends with it. The tales are linked together by their parallel episodes structured on the model of the quest. They differ mainly in the fact that the "Tale of Lancelot" is concerned with peace and unity, while the "Tale of Gareth" supplements these issues with the problems of justice and mercy in the realm.

The arch villains of Gareth's adventures, of whom the Red Knight of the Red Lands is the most vicious, are all characterized as being "wythouten mercy" or pity (232). The Red Knight has specifically directed his merciless acts (at the behest of a lady) against the Round Table, and it is to the Round Table that he is sent to ask mercy when he is finally subdued. Like the Tarquin episode in "The Tale of Lancelot," the hero proves his worthiness to be a member of the fellowship by asserting the appropriate Arthurian virtue in opposition to those who display the opposing vice. The merciless knight is subdued and granted mercy.

The goal of Gareth's acts is the glorification of Arthur and his Round Table. We have seen before that Malory displays the same concern as his contemporary, Fortescue, with the king's choice of members for the body politic. In *Le Morte Darthur* the council or Round Table is the instrument of Arthur's glorification. Not only do Gareth's actions glorify Arthur, but they win new members for the Round Table. Each of these recruits is presumably stripped of his envy and destructiveness and is thus suited for a fellowship bound together by loyalty.

In this highly idealized picture of Arthurian society in operation there is no hint of any internal weakness which the Arthurian code has not provided for. And although Malory makes Gareth's rejection of Gawain explicit in Tale IV, Gareth's reasons for shunning Gawain are based on that part of the code which forbids murder: "where he [Gawain] hated he wolde be avenged with murther and that hated Sir Gareth" (270). We have no indication as yet that Gawain's sin implicates the rest of the Round Table or is in any way a result of its weaknesses.

The major emphasis of Tales III and IV is on the power of loyalty to establish order and weld a fellowship of peers. The ideal remains intact, because it does not confront the internal difficulties involved in the members' relationships to each other. We can see here what was so compelling for a fifteenth-century man in the Round Table structure: it looks like the perfect fulfillment in reality of what John of Salisbury held could only exist on an ideal plane—a society of peers. It was John's contention that such a government was perfect for man only so long as he remained in a state of innocence. The last tales of *Le Morte Darthur* show the accuracy of John's admonition.

Tale V

In Malory's fifth tale, "The Tale of Tristram," the narrative changes pace and direction. The sprawling structure of this tale results partly from its function as the narrative middle which the French cycle lacks, and partly from its position as a transition between the state of the Arthurian ideal in Tales I-IV and its dissolution in Tales VI-VIII. I have chosen to discuss this tale in both Chapters 3 and 4 because of its transitional nature.

Unlike the fictional time of the first and last tales, the "Tristram" gains a disturbingly high degree of verisimilitude and reflects the structureless temporal nature of its French sources. It is in this framework that the narrative can turn to examine the daily operations of Arthurian society removed from the pressures of external crisis. We consequently find a new emphasis on the obligations of fellowship within the community in this tale. The best knights increase their worship as they act in accordance with the highest ideals of the community. Lancelot, Tristram, and Lamerok consistently gain stature because they attempt to increase the fame and worship of each other and of the Round Table as a whole. What R. M. Lumiansky has shown about Malory's conscious development of the trust and loyalty between Lancelot and Bors which begins in the "Tristram" section is relevant to other relationships as well.[31] Lamerok's character is greatly expanded from the source to emphasize his worthiness for fellowship with Tristram and Lancelot. The numerous parallels between Tristram and Lancelot (most often Malory's additions) set up a standard of communal bonds by which we are to judge all relationships within the Arthurian society. Here is the ideal society of peers indeed.

The last and most significant addition to Malory's Arthurian picture in Tale V is the very careful contrast between regal and political rule: the former being characteristic of Mark's court as Malory portrays it, and the latter of course

31. R. M. Lumiansky, "Malory's Steadfast Bors," *Tulane Studies in English*, VII (1958), 5-20.

of Arthur's domain. Critics who have found Malory's denigration of Mark's character a gratuitous element in his version of the "Tristram" have overlooked its function in the total definition of Arthur's government. Malory employs the contrast as the final touch in the Arthurian ideal, and he develops it in much the same way that Fortescue does in *De Legibus Angliae*.

When Fortescue drew his famous distinction between the governments of France and England, he grounded his interpretation of the English system in the reciprocal nature of king and polity set forth in the coronation oath. That the king was *under* the law and obliged to act for the common good is the central article in Fortescue's use of the coronation oath. As the model and guardian of eternal justice, the king must be devoted to the insurance of peace and the protection of his subjects from tyranny. Unity and peace are secured by law; the physiological metaphor of the mystical body politic is, as we have seen, devoted to establishing this point.

In turning to Malory we see that his version of the Tristram story hinges upon a contrast between the regal and absolute monarchy in Cornwall, where the arbitrary will of the king exposes the realm to dangers, and Arthur's domain where the king and his Round Table act for the common good and where the body politic is held together by the ligament of law. The numerous passages in which Mark behaves according to private whims and is rebuked by other knights have often been noted (e.g., 304, 408, 409, 431, 435). Most of these seem to be Malory's additions and several contain either direct or implicit comparisons between Mark and Arthur. We can see the whole political purpose of Malory's handling of Mark in this way in the story of Alexander the Orphan. Vinaver speculates that the original version of this story dwelt on the matter of a son's revenge for the death of his father.[32] The story certainly has all the earmarks of the typical medieval tale of the son's revenge for his father's death, but Malory has noticeably changed its emphasis in the

32. Vinaver, *Works of Malory*, III, 1486.

retelling. The episode in his version provides a moral on kingship.

We have seen earlier that the crucial issue for a political mind like Bracton's was the composition of the king's council or body politic. Arthur's court as Malory depicts it in Tales III and IV is almost wholly devoted to the recruitment and respect of the best knights of the realm. In the opening of "Alexander the Orphan" Mark acts directly against the interest of his realm by killing Bodwyne, who had rescued the kingdom from the Saracens. His motive of course is the specifically private one of envy. The consequence of Mark's behavior is that the best knights leave his kingdom, thus exposing it to both internal and external threats. Both peace and unity are sacrificed and this example shows very well that tyranny and peace are indeed mutually exclusive, as Fortescue had observed.

In accord with medieval English political theory, Mark's action costs him the allegiance of his knights. According to Bracton a king forfeits his kingship when he acts against justice and the common good. Upon hearing of Mark's treachery to Tristram, Sir Dynas rightfully declares his defiance of such a king and many knights follow suit (501–2). There is a general uprising in Cornwall against the king, and eventually he is imprisoned by his own knights. Mark has meddled with the sacred nature of the king's peace and justice; and Malory's definition of Mark's tyranny and treason arises from the dichotomy between tyranny on the one hand and peace and justice on the other, which we find in Bracton and Fortescue. For this reason Malory adds a passage indicating that it is illegitimate for the tyrant to plead for his sacred authority once he has violated the public sphere and in effect ceased to be king:

"Save my lyff," seyd kynge Marke, "and I woll make amendys. And concider that I am a kynge anoynted."

"Hit were the more shame," seyde sir Gaherys, "to save thy lyff! For thou arte a kynge anoynted with creyme, and therefore thou

sholdist holde with all men of worship. And therefore thou arte
worthy to dye" (408).

The Arthurian ideal thrives by the contrast with the court
of Mark in the "Tristram" section. Arthur's behavior is
that of the prince with an innate sense of equity; he functions as both judge and model: " 'A!' sayd sir Trystrams,
'ye know nat my lorde kynge Arthure, for all knyghtes may
lerne to be a kynght of hym' " (552). This and other comments which appear to be Malory's additions establish Arthur as the living model of the law. His central concern in
the "Tristram" is to attract the best knights of the realm
and weld them together into the political rule of peers.

We have now followed Malory as far as he is prepared to
go in his political idealization of Arthurian chivalry. The
contemporary political emphases are clear throughout his
revisions of his material, but they are soon to work differently
in the narrative. Instead of reinforcing the merits of Arthurian civilization as an historical model and a political
ideal, they begin in the last sections of Tale V through Tale
VIII to betray the shortcomings of the Arthurian code. Malory's idealization ebbs as the dangers of the Round Table's
own idealization of itself become more apparent. He allows
the contemporary political concerns which he has introduced
into the story to reveal that the Round Table represents only
an illusory fulfillment of Fortescue's political idealism and
in the most fundamental respect is a denial of that ideal.

The failure of Arthurian society lies mainly in its self-
deception and in its idealization of itself. The various ram-
ifications of this failure are reciprocal. Malory makes it
clear that Arthur's kingship is inadequately defined in its
public sphere, for one thing. The failures of his knights (and
I include the Lancelot-Guenevere adultery in this category)
are in part the result of Arthur's imperfect self-definition;
in themselves these failures would not be catastrophic, but
they are capable of destroying the society which is unprepared to recognize and deal with them. All personal issues

are permitted to become political issues, and the public sphere so precious to Fortescue and fifteenth-century political theory loses its autonomy.

Malory had arranged for this presentation of the tragedy as far back as the Balin story. His changes in the story have been subtle but crucial up to now, but as the plot of his sources turns to internal strife in Tale V he is free to bring his political insights to bear on the story. His version of the tragedy is sharpened by the degree of political idealism with which he initially presents King Arthur and his Round Table. Malory had to introduce a political ideal or model before he could lead us to judge the Round Table by the standards of that model. We understand the events of the last tales because the author has already educated us in matters of kingship and political morality.

4

The Arthurian Legend Exposed: Le Morte Darthur, Tales V–VIII

In turning to the collapse of the Arthurian ideal in *Le Morte Darthur*, we are forced to confront some problems related to the structure and nature of myth; such a consideration is crucial, since after all the Arthurian "myth" of social unity and cohesiveness disintegrates in these last tales. Only through some understanding of the function of myth can we see how this disintegration takes place in Malory's re-creation of the Arthurian story. The Lévi-Strauss structural approach to myth is based on the proposition that "mythical thought always progresses from the awareness of oppositions towards their resolution."[1] More specifically, he insists that myth exists for the very purpose of providing a "logical model capable of overcoming a contradiction."[2] This structuralist view of myth emphasizes its conservative nature: myth "tries to respect an older theory in the face of

1. Claude Lévi-Strauss, *Structural Anthropology* (New York, 1967), p. 221.
2. *Ibid.*, p. 226.

knowledge irreconcilable with it.''³ The contradictions and oppositions which the structuralist refers to are the antinomies basic to human existence. Lévi-Strauss gives the Oedipus myth as an example of the temporary reconciliation of the belief that man is autochthonous and the certain knowledge that he is born from the union of man and woman.

In the case of the Arthurian legend, the central contradiction which the story holds in check seems to lie in the fact that individuals are dependent on and drawn to the community and at the same time antisocial and antagonistic to its interests. The moral demands of Arthurian chivalry hold this contradiction in the balance, and the myth itself, because it cannot eliminate the antinomy in life, checks it in fiction. In Geoffrey, Wace, Layamon, and in the French and English romances before Malory, various interpretations surround the demise of the Arthurian world. But of these the Vulgate Cycle seems the only one to attribute the tragedy to *internal* causes, albeit spiritual ones. Despite this difference between the Vulgate romances and the other early versions, they all seem to have in common the presentation of the Arthurian legend as a model of social cohesion. In this sense the story functions for their various societies as a defense or reassurance against the threat of social disintegration; it plays, to a lesser or greater extent depending on the version, an exemplary role.

We can speculate from the evidence of the previous chapters that the Arthurian legend appealed to Malory because it had always served as a model of the cohesive society. We have seen a great deal of evidence that Malory enlarged upon the virtues of the story in this respect in Tales I–IV at least. But the crucial difference between Malory's version and the story as it appears in his sources is that while the sources present the Arthurian legend as a model for communal identity, they do so unconsciously; its exemplary role is *built in*, so to speak, and the romances do not acknowledge the pres-

3. Geoffrey Hartman, ''Structuralism: The Anglo-American Adventure,'' *Yale French Studies*, 36 and 37 (1966), 162.

ence of this function while they go about adding their own overlay of incidents and interpretations. With Malory, on the other hand, we find at first a purposeful and highly conscious exploitation of the story's role as a model of social cohesion. What was implicit in its sources becomes explicit in *Le Morte Darthur*. And it is this very conscious application of a political and social function to the story which in the end allows Malory to expose the myth of Arthurian society as a political ideal. The antinomies which the Arthurian legend in its earlier versions manages to reconcile are set free in the last tales of Malory's version. By allowing so great a degree of idealization to enter the initial stages of his story, Malory purposely disrupts the balance which allowed the ideal and the reality to exist without mutual betrayal in earlier versions.

In summing up this point we can turn back to an issue raised earlier concerning the cultural and political milieu of *Le Morte Darthur*. What we noted in Chapter 2 as being characteristic of Malory's time was its desperate concern for the permanence of human institutions in a time of crisis. With Fortescue this concern manifested itself in the need to define what characterizes England as a nation, who makes up this nation, and what continuity it maintains in time. Malory turns to art, and specifically to a national legend rich in its associations of social cohesion and communal identity, to examine such definitions. But by turning to the story as a potential cultural solution, in making it serve as a conscious cultural ideal, Malory—as we shall see—accomplished two things: he exposed the true nature of the moral demands implicit in Arthurian chivalry; and in showing their ultimate failure, he demonstrated the fallacy of consciously reviving the moral demands of the past to try to control the present.

A few general comments on the dissolution of the Arthurian ideal ought to illuminate those hidden aspects of the Arthurian story which Malory's version, by virtue of its special cultural demands, brings to light. The causality of the tragedy in Malory's book has usually been seen the wrong way around. That is, it has always been said that the tragedy results from a conflict of loyalties. But it becomes clear from reading the story in the way I have suggested that Malory is recording the decline of an institution, and the conflict of loyalties to God, king, and lady is not the cause but the *result* of the institution's losing its power to bind individuals to it and to prescribe what they shall give up in order to be so bound. In the last four tales we see that the Arthurian structure can no longer restrict the liberties of the knights with any success. What we should be interested in, then, is how and why the Arthurian institution forfeited its prescriptive powers.

The reasons which we can uncover for the dissolution of Arthurian society ultimately rest in its attitude towards its past and future. The immediate problems which beset Arthur have their sources in the earliest stages of his reign. Malory has reshaped the role of prophecy in the entire story so that it represents the constant threat of the past to reassert its power over the present. Merlin's prophecies in Malory's version are largely restricted to forecasting the consequences of certain events which happened in the early stages of Arthurian history. The begetting of Mordred, for instance, is an episode nearly buried in Arthur's past. It is so remote, in fact, that Arthur seems not only to have forgotten it, but also to have forgotten Merlin's prophecy relating to it. In fact all the crucial elements in the downfall of the Arthurian world have their roots in the past which Arthur has forgotten: the Lot-Pellinore feud, the choice of Guenevere and the Lancelot-Guenevere prophecy, and the Balin prophecies all are pre-Round Table, and all exemplify the past reasserting itself and controlling the present.

We can now see the reason Malory eliminated the role which fate or fortune plays in his sources. The prophecies are simply used here to record the claims of the past on the present, and the Arthurian world can therefore be held responsible for not coming to terms with its past. In failing to heed prophecies, and thereby implicitly denying the influence and importance of his past, Arthur has failed to control it, and thereby eliminated the possibility of his future.

Underlying this disregard for the dangers of its past, there is another element fundamental to the demise of the Round Table: its overevaluation of its own powers. The source of this exaggeration of its strengths is undoubtedly to be found in the idealism of Arthurian chivalry. Because of its asceticism and altruism chivalry seems the perfect historical ideal, given the political aspirations of Malory's time. But Malory's narrative discloses that the institution has asked more from the individual members of the Round Table in the way of renouncing private interests and of mutual devotion than is either realistic or safe. Conflicting loyalties exist in all societies; they are not in any way peculiar to the Round Table. What is distinctive about this structure is that its chivalric code, in an attempt to keep such conflicts under control, has repressed them almost out of sight by idealizing itself and exaggerating the loyalty of the Round Table knights to each other. Arthurian society, as a result of such excessive idealization of itself, has lost sight of the dangerous impulses of self-interest and has set free other destructive impulses which are unrecognized by the group. The specific problems which arise within the Arthurian structure in the last four tales suggest that we are faced with a society which as a result of such excessive idealization of its own powers is living psychologically beyond its means; it is asking more of its members than it can return to them in the way of personal stability and fulfillment. The change from the paternal or regal society of Uther to the fraternal political society of Arthur's Round Table has meant that the Round Table society must generate *within itself* the disciplines, renunciations and restraints which in the former age were imposed externally by the ruler. We should therefore look for the source of Malory's tragedy in the idealism which led Arthurian society to proceed without equalizing these pressures of social cohesion and individual instincts, and in its failure to provide itself with internal restraints.

Malory brings out the point that the confusion which confronts the political structure of the Round Table is a result of Arthur's ambiguous position as the "leader" of an ideally *fraternal* society. Medieval political theory, however visionary it became in advocating a society of peers and a political rule, never wavered in its demand for a strong leader. We have seen how Malory had stressed in Arthur those qualities which thinkers from John of Salisbury through Bracton and Fortescue had advocated as best suited for kingship. The king is the head of the body politic of which his councilors or his parliament are the limbs. He is not simply *primus inter pares* as we have seen, because in his public person he participates in a different time scale and is the representative of sacred things. In the last tales of Malory's book, however, we discover first that the real and significant distinctions between the king's public body and private person have not been preserved in Arthur's kingship, and second that as a result of this failure his kingship cannot survive the loss of his fellowship.

The psychological soundness of a theory like that of the king's twinned being stems from the unambiguous role of the leader's *persona publica*; only by maintaining this public person, as opposed to the *privata voluntas*, can the leader maintain the emotional ties which hold this group together. The communal identity of one member with another is established initially by the relation which each member has to the leader. We find in Malory's version of the Arthurian legend that in crisis situations the dissolution of the society results from Arthur's failure to differentiate between his public and private roles. He cannot define himself except in terms of his followers, and he therefore becomes subject to the personal emotional ties which characterize his knights' relationships with each other. As a result, the crises of Tale VIII, no matter how minimal the actual danger, result in group panic—the knights lose their faith in Arthur and then necessarily abandon their attachments to each other.

The last general statement about the collapse of the Arthurian ideal in the final tales of *Le Morte Darthur* involves Malory's position in relation to his readers. Malory's fifteenth-century audience, of whom Caxton must be typical, is described by Margaret Schlauch as a wealthy merchant class which had superseded the old aristocratic families depleted by the Wars of the Roses.[4] If so, and if these are the "many noble and dyvers gentylmen" who requested that Caxton print Malory's stories, their interest in imitating in art and life the tastes and activities of their predecessors (who were also their superiors) is certainly understandable. By repeating the customs and culture of the aristocracy they become the masters of the social situation which had formerly mastered them. Whether we accept this explanation or the explanation that the interest in Malory's Arthuriad represents the functionless aristocracy reviving a tradition with which to comfort itself, we are faced in both instances with the question of a conscious cultural *revival*.

Malory himself is of course conscious of the archaism of his work. He occasionally indicates his historical perspective by referring to the Arthurian customs "in tho dayes." References of this sort are especially frequent in the last two tales, where his ability to make Arthurian chivalry serve realistic contemporary ends is greatly reduced. As the fragility of Arthurian society is exposed in Tales VI, VII, and VIII, the cultural gap becomes more pronounced. The basic problem is one that Auerbach noted in his essay on romance society in *Mimesis*: "Courtly culture gives rise to the idea that nobility, greatness, and intrinsic values have nothing in common with everyday reality."[5] Here is the heart of chivalry's inadequacy as an historical ideal of life. Malory has tested the ideal as a source of stable government and social

4. Margaret Schlauch, *English Medieval Literature and its Social Foundations* (Warsaw, 1956), p. 285.
5. Erich Auerbach, *Mimesis* (New York, 1957), p. 122.

relations, and in the last three tales it is clear that if its illusory world of romance is pressed too far into the service of actual needs, the ideal betrays itself. What has happened is that the moral background and function of the legend which we spoke of as implicit in Malory's sources have been made too explicit in his book. We are in the end faced with the futility of reviving a tradition and a morality and imposing them from the outside on a later age. By the end Malory has shown so much about what makes Arthurian society operate that it can not be morally compelling for his own time.

Tale V

In the second half of "The Tale of Tristram" we see further evidence of Malory's critical awareness as narrator. Here his additions to the story are most often expositions of Round Table society as it should be and/or disclosures of it as it is. At this point in the narrative the Arthurian world is unified and external threats have been reduced to a few forays with occasional outsiders: "And at that tyme kynge Arthure regned, and he was hole kynge of Ingelonde, Walys, Scotlonde, and of many othir realmys. Howbehit there were many kynges that were lordys of many contreyes, but all they helde their londys of kynge Arthure" (276).[6] The Round Table has so to speak run out of enemies, and the narrative turns to the preoccupations of Arthurian society with itself. There is a consequent emphasis on tournaments, reputations, and personal relationships.

The shortcomings of the Arthurian code of Tale I become apparent only in the context of the community at peace, because the code is primarily directed at the knight's obligations to the society *outside* the Round Table. The code is inadequate as stated in Tale I because, as we learn in Tales V–VIII, Arthur is incapable of looking beyond the demands

6. This and all subsequent page references to *Le Morte Darthur* refer to Eugene Vinaver (ed.), *The Works of Sir Thomas Malory* (Oxford, 1954).

of a present situation to recognize and anticipate the internal weaknesses of his fellowship. Vinaver notices the differences between "Malory's" code and the one in the source, and decides that Malory was not concerned with the spiritual nature of Arthur's fellowship.[7] It seems clear from these last three tales, however, that the code is of Arthur's making and characteristic of his approach to things. In this context we realize that it was *Arthur* who was not sufficiently interested in the internal and spiritual problems which confront a political body. At the end of Tale V and in Tales VI–VIII the hostility which Arthur's knights had formerly directed at outsiders had no object except the Round Table itself. The extreme civility and asceticism of chivalry cannot help but store up a residue of aggression which, robbed of a legitimate enemy, will express itself in antisocial form.

It is not surprising that a direct relationship develops between the degree of Arthur's control as king and the nature of the personal relationships within the fellowship. The perceptible decline in Arthur's charisma expresses itself in the lack of trust between members of the Round Table themselves. The episode of the Red City functions as a last warning to Arthur that the beneficent king is by no means invulnerable to the treachery of those he trusts. King Harmance's tragedy is a direct result first of his naiveté, and secondly of his insistence on following a personal or private whim and ignoring the future of his realm. The moral of the story is stated in the form of a warning to Arthur's court: " 'Therefore all the astatys and lordys, of what astate ye be, loke ye beware whom ye take aboute you. And therefore, sir, and ye be a knyght of kynge Arthurs courte remembir this tale' " (527).

Other warnings to the Round Table are stated in a still more explicit way. Throughout the tale the Round Table is concerned with attracting to it three knights who are among the best in the realm, Tristram, Palomydes, and Lamerok.

---

7. Eugene Vinaver (ed.), *The Works of Sir Thomas Malory* (Oxford, 1947), III, 1320.

The Round Table's success here is dependent first on Arthur's appeal as a leader, and secondly upon his exercise of enough authority to stabilize the relationships among his knights so that their society is safe for others. By the end of the tale it is clear that Arthur cannot function strongly enough as a leader to stabilize his fellowship. In a long passage added by Malory, Lancelot and Lamerok discuss the safety of Arthur's court (488). Lamerok departs from the fellowship because he recognizes that there has been a collapse in the mutual trust among the knights. Lancelot tells him that Arthur will command Gawain and his clan not to harm him. Arthur had formerly promised Lamerok by his crown to protect him from Gawain (494). But Lamerok realizes that Arthur is no longer in a position to re-establish trust and safety; thus despite Lancelot's suggestion he leaves. Malory makes a great deal more than do his sources of Lamerok's murder by Gawain and his brothers. It is symptomatic for him of Arthur's failure to use his kingship to prevent the distrust and panic which results in both murder and the dissolution of the bonds of fellowship. In a seemingly original passage Tristram expresses just this sentiment on Lamerok's murder (514), and soon thereafter we find Tristram commenting on the effect of the incident: " 'And for suche thynges,' seyde sir Trystrams, 'I feare to drawe unto the courte of kyng Arthure' " (520).

Through Malory's use of the murder of Lamerok we begin to see that the treason, envy and revenge of Gawain and his brothers implicates the entire Arthurian structure. What begins as personal vendetta ends in the envy and hatred of Arthurian virtues in general. Aggravayne and Mordred, in *le Roman de Tristan* have a grievance against Dinaden because his father killed the father of their friend, Dalan: but Malory's version glosses over their motives in order to represent them as willfully destructive of goodness. At this point Malory adds a forecast of their murder of Dinaden during the quest. It is clear from Malory's special use of Dinaden and his omission of a motive for Aggravayne and Mordred

that he sees the attitudes and actions of these latter to stand
not for personal revenge, but for the complete perversion of
the Arthurian value system: ''Whan they [Aggravayne and
Mordred] undirstode that hit was Sir Dynadan they were
more wrothe than they were before, for they haited hym oute
of measure bycause of sir Lameroke. For Sir Dynadan had
suche a custom that he loved all good knyghtes that were
valyaunte, and he hated all tho that were destroyers of good
knyghtes. And there was none that haited Sir Dynadan but
tho that ever were called murtherers'' (461).

The entire characterization of Dinaden differs markedly
from the prose *Tristan* where he is the irreverent mocker of
all aspects of chivalric life. Critics usually attribute Malory's
omission of much of this irony to his desire to preserve the
high seriousness of knighthood. But Malory's indictment of
chivalry is if anything more pointed than that in his sources,
and he has simply sharpened the character of Dinaden as a
way of hitting at the particular aspects of chivalry which
are potentially disruptive to the community. Dinaden's rid-
icule of courtly love and his long diatribes on insignificant
chivalric customs are obviously irrelevant for this purpose,
and Malory has omitted them. These omissions leave only
two aspects of Dinaden's character in Malory's version. First
he is consistently portrayed as devoid of pride and envy, the
inspiration of love and trust for other good knights. Second,
his comments on cowardice and his reluctance to fight appear
in Malory's account when it is clear that the conventions of
knight errantry work against the ideal of fellowship:

"Not so," seyde Sir Dynadan, "for I have no wyll to juste."
"Wyth me shall ye juste," seyde the knyght, "or that ye passe
this way."
"Sir, whether aske you justys *of love othir of hate*?" (452, Italics
mine.)

At another point he at first refuses to help Aggravayne and
Mordred because he doubts the justice of their cause. When
the odds are overwhelming, he argues for the addition of

wisdom to valor by ridiculing the chivalric excesses of Tristram, Lancelot, and Palomydes. In this use of Dinaden Malory's critical awareness of the paradoxes of Arthurian idealism is apparent.

That the full significance of Dinaden's actions and comments is not apparent to the rest of the Round Table is attributable to Malory's dramatic sense in handling the tragedy. The suspense of the final tales derives from this pattern established in the Tristram section: the method by which the fellowship destroys itself develops more rapidly than the awareness that it is being destroyed. Similarly, Malory's ideal as it appears through his use of Dinaden anticipates the criticisms of chivalry in the "Quest," while the Arthurian code enables the Round Table to remain ignorant of the abuses of chivalry. Malory has shown in this tale that although the existing ideals of Arthurian society are responsible for the achievements of the Round Table, they are at the same time inadequate and therefore partly responsible for the dissolution of the community.

In discussing the conventions of courtly love in the Tristram legend, Denis de Rougemont comments on their role in the shape of the plot: "It is precisely the arbitrary character of the obstructions introduced into a tale that may show what this tale is really about and what is the real nature of the passion it is concerned with."[8] Here he is referring to the illogical complications which the conventions of courtly love introduce to sustain the agony of the lovers in spite of the fact that there are realistic opportunities for Tristram and Isolde to live happily ever after. In Malory the conventions of chivalry replace those of courtly love as "arbitrary obstructions." In countless episodes the knights seek peril for its own sake: close friends and brothers fight each other "without knowing" it when it would have been perfectly easy to reveal their identities to each other and thereby avoid both the fight and their ensuing remorse (e.g., 359, 401,

8. Denis de Rougemont, *Love in the Western World* (New York, 1940), p. 38.

425, 485, 571, 603). All challenges must be met and all fellows must be revenged, making it almost impossible not to
do battle in a wrongful cause. The debate on wisdom and
valor which Malory inserts throughout the book (e.g., 432,
521) implies that the two Arthurian ideals are mutually exclusive. Dinaden mocks the chivalric conventions because they
begin to act as fate directing the behavior of even the best
knights who unwittingly wound and humiliate each other.
Tournaments and battles by the end of Tale V cease to be
simply ''war games'' and become occasions for family pride
and envy with the same risks and casualties as war itself.
There is a noticeable deterioration in the feeling and the
goals from the early tournaments of the tale to the tournament
at Lonezep, where many knights of the Round Table take
sides against Arthur because by doing so they can win more
worship. Finally, near the end of the tale in a passage presumably original with Malory, Lancelot rebukes his kin for
their treasonous plot to slay Tristram because his reputation
had temporarily replaced the name of Lancelot (581). If
we ask the same question about these chivalric conventions
which Denis de Rougemont does of courtly conventions, we
must ultimately discover that the highly ordered rituals of
chivalry disguise a passion for anarchy, fratricide, and revenge. Surely much of the appeal of the story of Arthur
lies in the paradoxes it temporarily holds in check: the highly
ordered ritualistic society of peers devoted to a charismatic
leader, and the anarchy, fratricide, and cuckolding of the
king. These aspects of Arthurian society revealed in Tale V
have taken us some distance from Fortescue's cohesive political model.

Tale VI

We have seen that in the first tales Malory defines the
Arthurian ideal in political terms and emphasizes the success with which it maintained itself against external threats.
In the narrative middle of *Le Morte Darthur*, the ''Tristram,'' it appears that the Arthurian code as it was form-

ulated in Tale I has not defined the knights' responsibilities for the internal unity of the Round Table; here the fellowship shows itself insufficient to withstand the antisocial pressures which underly its version of chivalry. The decline in fortune in the last tales is plotted against the gradual disclosure that the fellowship is also unprepared for—and therefore inadequate to meet—the needs of the individual.

The Grail quest is in this sense the turning point of the book; it reveals that the Round Table has impoverished itself as a group ideal by neglecting both the spiritual ties between members and the spiritual resources of each individual. The adventures of the quest as Malory presents them demonstrate that the Round Table as an institution has lost its power to coerce its members. The knights are after all supposed to achieve the Grail for the glory of the Round Table, but their actions betray the fact that they have lost their sense of relationship with the Arthurian fellowship. The quest in Tale VI becomes a metaphor of societal dissolution, whereas in Tales III and IV it had functioned as a metaphor of unity. Without the structure of the fellowship the individual knights experience a sense of isolation and insecurity which precipitates the dissolution of the Round Table. As a panic measure they realign themselves into smaller groups in the "Quest" instead of proceeding as individuals, and these splinter groups become in Tales VII and VIII the agents of destruction.

The failure in the "Quest" has yet another dimension which is also related to medieval political theory. In Tale VI we see the consequences of Arthur's neglect of the moral and sacred purpose of the state which John of Salisbury had emphasized as the primary obligation of the king. The immortality of the state in fifteenth-century political theory was intimately connected with the semi-religious terminology used to describe it, and—as we shall see—the quest for the Grail in Malory's Arthuriad seems to be designed to establish at this belated stage such a spiritual basis for the Round Table. Whereas the French *Queste* is essentially a universalized exposition on grace and salvation, Malory confines his version to the specific failures and successes of Arthur's knights, so that the "Quest" becomes a specific commentary on the failure of Arthurian society to preserve itself by spiritual means.

What Malory omits from his source are the large portions of purely theological material on grace and salvation. As a result of this method, those French passages concerning the failure of the fellowship which do remain in *Le Morte Darthur* are thrown into a sharper focus. The experience of the quest tests the spiritual resources of the individual; one cannot see the Grail in the company of others. The substance of the hermits' explanations which remain in Malory's account emphasize that the Round Table's existence as a group ideal has seriously impoverished its members as individuals; the Arthurian code has not provided the knights with the individual virtues of patience and humility necessary for the spiritual quest. And it is the very deficiency of such qualities which in turn causes the individuals to panic, to betray and desert Arthur in the last tale. The commentary on Gawain's dream (683), for instance, is so pointed that it is difficult to believe that Malory did not borrow it and others like it for their pertinence to his theme. Malory's "Grail" is very compact, and what remains from the French must have been chosen specifically for its thematic relevance. Even Arthur's tears and the tone of sorrow at the departing which Vinaver and Moorman call Malory's addition,[9] are present in the French version.[10] Obviously, then, this passage is not simply inserted to show Arthur's attachment to his knights; in both versions of the "Quest" it functions as our first indication that the fellowship will not survive the spir-

9. Vinaver, *Works of Malory*, III, 1535; Charles Moorman, "The Tale of the Sangreall," *Malory's Originality*, ed. R. M. Lumiansky (Baltimore 1964), p. 203.

10. H. Oskar Sommer (ed.), *The Vulgate Version of the Arthurian Romances*: VI, *Les Adventures Ou La Queste del Saint Graal* (Carnegie Institute, 1913), p. 20, 1. 8. This passage and one immediately following it describe Arthur's tears and the tone of grief at the parting.

itual demands made on its members. In addition, this passage also emphasizes the fact that Arthur's office as king is inextricably bound up with the fate of the Round Table.

It must be emphasized, however, that Malory presents the "Quest" as the Round Table's one opportunity to preserve itself. The Grail appears at the outset, and in a sourceless line Malory says that by its light "eyther saw other, by their semynge, fayrer than ever they were before" (634). This transitory revelation holds out to the Round Table the possibility of a harmonious political fellowship re-established through the spiritual fulfillment of each individual. Malory's chief alterations from the French appear, therefore, in his treatment of the Round Table before the departure, and in the trials of its greatest failure, Lancelot. These changes emphasize that the failure to take this instance of grace as a warning is attributable to that knight's lack of preparation for individual responsibility, to his insufficient knowledge of spiritual matters, and to his misunderstanding of the distinction between this quest and any other.

Gawain's naive vow to follow the Grail in Malory differs from the French source, where he at least exhibits some knowledge of the tremendous importance of the Grail's appearance as a sign of grace. His speech in the French is longer, less impetuous, and more humble than that in Malory, where he does not mention the grace that has been given them. In Malory Gawain's enthusiasm stems from his curiosity alone; he wants to see what the Grail looks like. In Malory it is Gawain, not Galahad, who sets the tone of the quest. In the source Bagdemagnus insists that Galahad is the spiritual leader who must vow first and show the others the way: "Sire fait le rois baudemagnus [au Roi] sauue vostre grace il ne le fera mie premierement. Mais grace il ne le fera auant nous tous qui nos deuons tenir por maistre a seignor de la table roonde ce est galaad."[11] This passage and the ensuing vows are not in Malory, nor are the knights

11. *Ibid.*, p. 18, 1. 18.

confessed as the priest recommends. They depart with their former ideals and sins still intact.

Gawain persists in conducting himself as though he were on his way to a tournament and continually adopts companions who wonder why they never have any adventures. Malory retains Galahad's remarks to Ywain and others about the necessity of proceeding alone and reinforces them by an alteration in a hermit's speech to Gawain. In the French, the hermit rebukes Gawain for murdering the seven brothers without giving them a chance to repent. Malory omits this aspect of the speech and substitutes instead the hermit's distinction between Galahad who subdued the brothers (the seven deadly sins) by "hymself alone," and Gawain who with his two companions murdered them. Malory is naturally interested in keeping the characterization of Gawain as a murderer in the forefront, but the murder is only possible because Gawain is incapable of proceeding alone (650–51).

The indictment of chivalric customs and their connection with fratricide, which began in the latter half of the "Tristram" section, receives special emphasis in Malory's version of the Grail legend. For Malory, fratricide seems to be the central symbol of societal dissolution. His whole revision of the Balin story as a moral vignette was centered on the unwitting combat of the two brothers. The "Quest" begins with an echo of this story: according to Malory (but not to his source) Galahad's sword is the same one that Balin used in killing his brother (632). The emphasis on fratricide reappears when Gawain kills Ywain by mistake, and the author makes the comment that in future days it will be told that one sworn brother killed another. Ywain's reminder that as knights of the Round Table they were "sworne togydir," and his message to Arthur to remember him "for olde brothirhode" (682) seem also to be Malory's additions. Finally, the whole episode concerning Bors and Lyonell, his brother, receives a different emphasis in Malory's version where Lyonell is described as a murderer and a traitor to brotherhood.

In the source he is simply characterized as deficient in Christian virtue.

In another place (643), a good man explains to Galahad the allegory of the tomb he has just seen. In the French Galahad receives a long sermon on the tomb and the body and voice which emerged from it. All three tokens are essential to an understanding of the incident in the French. Malory, however, omits the explanation of the body and the voice, leaving a rather pointed emphasis on the moral of the tomb by itself: ". . . hit betokenyth the duras of the worlde. . . . For there was suche wrecchydnesse that the fadir loved nat the sonne, nother the sonne loved nat the fadir" (643). Here the violation of family ties pertains to fathers and sons. The disturbance of this crucial relationship recurs in the Percival section where the author comments on the singularity of Percival's virtue at a time when "the sonne spared nat the fadir no more than a straunger" (664).

The most significant thematic alterations from the source occur in connection with Lancelot. Far from exalting Lancelot, these alterations underline his lack of preparation for spiritual matters and attribute this failing both directly and indirectly to the ideals of the Round Table. Unlike the author of the French *Queste* Malory delays Lancelot's understanding of his spiritual responsibility until the end of "The Morte Arthur." This lack of understanding or wisdom is not characteristic of Lancelot in the French version, because his spiritual failure there is not intended to be symptomatic of the weaknesses of Arthur's communal code. Malory does not excuse chivalry. His "Grail" is if anything a more severe indictment of the chivalric code than the French *Queste*. Lancelot's instability is his sin in Malory, not because Malory wants to ignore adultery or to let Lancelot off easily, but because his society has not provided him with a consistent code for governing himself in spiritual matters. Lancelot's experience at the Grail chapel differs significantly in this respect from its source, where Lancelot understands what is required of him. Malory emphasizes Lancelot's naiveté and bewilderment. He leaves the chapel weeping "for than he demed never to have worship more"; he contrasts his humiliation with his former glory and, finally, he is easily comforted by the birds singing around him. In the French, Lancelot's first two responses do not appear, and the birds serve only to remind him of his sin and failure: "Car lu ou il quidoit ioie trouer & toute honor terriene [la] a il failli ce est as auentures del saint graal."[12] The naiveté of Lancelot's reactions is peculiar to Malory's account. It seems perfectly designed to emphasize that the ideals of his society are the sources of his instability and his ignorance.

When the hermit explains Lancelot's experience at the Grail chapel to him, Malory takes another opportunity to stress Lancelot's lack of preparation for his trial. In the French Lancelot is rebuked for wasting the gifts God gave him. In Malory, the hermit adds that Lancelot is shamed for bringing himself sinful and unconfessed into the presence of holiness. Immediately following this admonition Malory omits the passage where the hermit promises Lancelot that God will make him successful in all endeavors if he will only give up Guenevere. For Malory such a solution would only undermine the severity of Lancelot's other sins and their pertinence to the faults of the whole Round Table; therefore he omits it. In fact, Malory's insistence on Lancelot's instability implies that if it is not the cause of his pride and adultery, it is at least the reason for his persistence in ignorance and consequently sin.

Malory's shift away from the specific sin of adultery as Lancelot's main weakness to an emphasis on the more general instability which characterizes Lancelot and his society is again evident in Book IV of his "Quest." In Malory's eyes Lancelot's adultery and the courtly love motif are simply the antisocial results of a more basic problem in Arthurian society: that is, the instability of the individual as well as his confusion of personal and social responsibilities is germane to all of Arthurian society. In the French, prior to

12. *Ibid.*, p. 45, 11. 10–12.

Lancelot's vision the hermit explains that Lancelot entered knighthood completely virtuous and well fortified against sin and continued so until the devil devised Guenevere as the only possible temptation. The hermit goes on to speculate on the great deeds Lancelot might have done had it not been for the adultery. Obviously, Malory omits this passage to heighten the importance of the more general moral in the vision which follows it, where the substance of the old man's admonition is a reminder that knighthood should be informed by spiritual concerns. In the French text the old man merely commands the knight to yield up his treasure. Malory's expansion of this passage and his omission of the one on adultery accord perfectly with his method of using Lancelot's experience to illuminate the more basic weakness of the Round Table as a whole and to show the spiritual basis upon which the fellowship must be reconstructed to survive.

These alterations in the nature of Lancelot's sin are reinforced and clarified by the hermit's speech on the tournament of Black and White knights. The French version uses this contest as a figurative recapitulation of Lancelot's experience in the quest thus far, and it appears that he has made considerable spiritual progress. In Malory, however, the contest is an actual tournament which takes place immediately after Lancelot has been admonished in the vision to use prowess for spiritual ends. Malory's version emphasizes Lancelot's instability; his chivalric code prompts him to join the sinners without allowing him to perceive the relation between this test and the spiritual lesson which preceded it. At the end of this passage the Lancelot of the French *Queste* exhibits his theological sophistication by admitting that after these lessons he must hold himself fully responsible for any further sin. He then has a short adventure in the wilderness where his fortitude and patience demonstrate that he has understood his experience. Malory omits these two passages because his Lancelot never even realizes that individual responsibility is the question at hand.

Bors' partial success in the ''Quest'' is carefully counterpointed against Lancelot's failure. Malory has purposely developed Bors' character in the previous tales to show his unwavering adherence to the ideals of fellowship as they have been presented to him *before* his spiritual adventure. It is quite important to note, then, that Bors' success in the "Quest" is dependent upon his temporary denial of Arthurian customs: he forsakes his own brother in his pursuit of a higher goal. Later, in a speech original with Malory, Bors demonstrates his understanding that his own spiritual stability is contingent upon his rejection of the code: " 'fayre brother, God knowith myne entente, for ye have done full evyll thys day to sle an holy pryste which never trespasced. Also ye have slayne a jantill knyght, and one of oure felowis. And well wote ye that I am nat aferde of you gretely, but I drede the wratthe of God; and thys ys an unkyndely werre' " (701). There is a second dimension of this speech which indicates Bors' role in the quest. He acts as a link between the spiritual fellowship of Galahad and Percivale and the earthly fellowship of the Round Table. Spiritual stability becomes important to him as a way of preventing crimes against "one of oure fellowis." Bors' stability is composed of the individual will and faith which should have been the basis of Arthur's code. Lancelot's instability lies in his inclination to act according to the destructive *collective* code which prompted him to join the Black Knights.

The theme of stability is Malory's way of making the quest pertinent to his political themes. Individual stability in spiritual matters is essential to the stability of a worldly ideal. Because the Round Table is established without accounting for these matters, it is at least partly responsible for the failure of its knights in the Grail quest, and almost totally responsible for its own dissolution at the end. Clearly, the final additions to the quest purposely emphasize the solitary deaths of the Grail winners who relinquish the claims of an earthly fellowship which will be unable to resist disorder. Galahad's message to Lancelot is then a *momento mori* for the entire Round Table: " 'My fayre lorde, salew me unto my lorde Sir Launcelot, my fadir, and as sone as ye se hym bydde hym remembir of *this worlde unstable'* " (739, Italics mine.). Bors returns. In the last tales his experience is designed to show the incompatibility of spiritual ideals in the framework of the Arthurian ideal.

Tale VII

The last two tales work out the consequences of the failures initiated in the previous action. Nowhere is the gap between Malory's political ideal and the actual behavior of the Round Table so great as in ''The Tale of Lancelot and Guenevere.'' Though critics have often assumed that this tale functions as Malory's last fling with the glories of Arthuriana, his alterations in the sources and his two major additions, ''The Great Tournament'' and ''The Healing of Sir Urry,'' direct our attention instead to the flowering of those disruptive tendencies which emerged in Tales V and VI.

The most notable change in the Arthurian society of Tale VIII, ''Lancelot and Guenevere,'' is in the attitude of the fellowship towards Arthur. Before the quest Arthur is idealized by his knights in several sourceless passages as the king and knight *par excellence*. In the Quest, the feeling of solidarity which such affection had produced breaks down: with their leader absent the knights lose their sense of communal identity and regroup themselves into smaller units. In Tale VI this development reflects a change in their relationships to the fellowship, but in Tale VII it is clear that the experience of the quest has also affected their attitude towards Arthur. The excessive idealization of Arthur as both fellow and king had very effectively covered the occasional envy and distrust which the knights quite naturally feel for their leader. Arthurian society has again endangered itself by over-idealizing its capacity to rid itself of internal strife. When the envy and distrust of Arthur do appear directly it is too late for the fellowship to handle them judiciously.

The source of distrust and hostility is in the very structure of Arthurian society. Arthur's authority is largely based on the degree of affection which he commands from his knights. But, as we see in Tales VII and VIII, the knights in turn demand thait he love them equally, and they are continually testing Arthur's fidelity to this ideal. Tale II seems to be primarily devoted to showing how well Arthur satisfies this demand as a way of demonstrating his fitness to be king. But in the long run, as the last two tales show, Arthur cannot hold himself apart from the personal aspects of the Round Table—that is, he cannot distinguish between the public and private aspects of his role, and as a result he is betrayed into partiality.

In Tale VII the lack of faith in Arthur is merely incipient, whereas in the last tale it appears fullblown. The first evidences of this attitude occur in the "Poisoned Apple" episode. Malory adds Madore's speech to Arthur on the subject of Guenevere's trial for treachery (748). Madore does not take Arthur's word on the innocence of the queen but reminds Arthur that although he is a king he is also bound by the same ties of knighthood as his fellows and therefore should understand their insistence on having Guenevere brought to trial. Bors immediately understands the implications of such a trial for Arthur's kingship, and in a speech original with Malory points out the knights' lack of respect for their king: " 'Weite you well, my fayre lordis, hit were shame to us all and we suffird to se the moste noble quene of the worlde to be shamed opynly, consyderyng her lorde and oure lorde ys the man of moste worship crystyhde, and he hath ever worshipped us all in all placis' " (751).

The other piece of evidence which shows the perceptible weakening of Arthur's position as king lies in the implication of Lancelot's affair with Guenevere. Courtly love is given a strong political dimension in Malory's version of the story. Lancelot's adultery with Guenevere is first of all his contribution to the general abandonment of Arthur. Furthermore, his affair represents a withdrawal from the fellowship. As Malory portrays it in Tale VII, courtly love is essentially antisocial, because the two lovers relinquish their need for the rest of the society. The tournaments of Tale VII all show Lancelot pitting himself *against* Arthur's side, and his antisocial behavior is always related to the state of his worship in Guenevere's eyes. By contrast, Malory adds a section describing Gareth's modesty, generosity, and loyalty—virtues which Lancelot has ceased to display under the conditions of the tournament. The poignancy of the story in Malory's account is very largely the result of the tension which he highlights between Lancelot's very real affection for Arthur and devotion to his fellows and his hostility to both in his behavior throughout the last two tales. Earlier versions seem to have kept this tension out of sight, and it is only Malory's insistence on the political themes of the story which forces these oppositions to our attention.

Taking the five episodes of Tale VII in order we can see the extent to which Malory has exposed the political reality of Arthurian society and revealed its inappropriateness as an historical ideal of life. His additions and changes here not only expose Arthurian society to sharper criticism than we find in the sources, but they also reveal that its weaknesses are not the result of a gradual decay, but were built into the structure. In this way the book is made to function quite obviously as a *moral* for its author's age.

The additions in the opening of the first episode purposely link it very closely in time to the end of the Quest in order to tighten the cause and effect relationship between the two tales. In the first conversation between Lancelot and Guenevere Malory's additions indicate that whatever misgivings he may have about the adultery, Lancelot has not been slow to make up for lost time. Furthermore, his remarks on his failure in the Quest reveal his continued ignorance that his adultery is ultimately related to a larger complex of sins which affect the entire Round Table. These additions prepare the reader for Lancelot's behavior at the end of the episode where he defends his promise to be Guenevere's knight ''in ryght othir in wrong'' (755, Malory's addition)—an ironic echo both of his confessions in the quest and the vow he and his fellows make each Pentecost to "take no batayles in wrongefull quarell for no love ne for no worldis goodis" (91).

Finally, Lancelot's instability in this episode is only one aspect of disorder in the Round Table. The motivation for the poisoning of Gawain, unexplained in the source, establishes that the spiritual interlude between "The Tale of Tristram" and "The Tale of Lancelot and Guenevere" has not altered the course of revenge and disaster. The gradual relaxation of the political ties which had bound the knights to Arthur before the Quest necessarily culminates in this mutual distrust of the followers themselves. Malory's version of the "Poisoned Apple" is a highly condensed statement about the causal relationship between the events of the Quest and the events which follow it. In the Quest the Arthurian political structure confronts the problem of fratricide through the metaphorical explanations of the hermits; in the "Poisoned Apple" the threat of fratricide is a literal one, and moreover this threat is indicative of the fact that self-destruction is an integral part of the Arthurian brotherhood.

Malory's additions to the second episode stress the unfulfilled promise of the Arthurian ideal. Accompanying this theme is the indication that we are now some distance in time from the glorious days of the Round Table. This commentary on the action is presented in the sourceless speech of an old hermit who is asked to heal the disguised Lancelot: " 'I have seyne the day,' seyde the ermyte, 'I wolde have loved hym [Lancelot] the worse because he was ayenste my lorde kynge Arthure, for sometyme I was one of the felyship. But now, *I thanke God, I am othirwyse disposed*' " (765, italics mine.). This addition echoes the themes of the Quest by underlining the general collapse of faith in and loyalty to both Arthur and the fellowship of the Round Table. The irony that the disguised knight whom the holy man is asked to cure is actually the first knight of the Round Table adds another dimension of absurdity and disorder to

the anarchical behavior of Arthur's fellowship and sets the
tone for the next episode, which is original with Malory.

"The Great Tournament" seems a necessary addition to
the tale at this point because it is the fullest presentation thus
far of the fellowship at work destroying itself, and simultaneously it includes Arthur's *first* complete definition of
the internal obligations of fellowship. In accordance with
the dramatic development of action and theme in the previous tales, Arthur's definition of the ideal changes to meet
the demands made upon it; it does not anticipate them, and
consequently the ideal appears in Arthur's speech to Gareth
after the initial damage has been done. Similarly, the final
component of the definition—the responsibility of the individual for his spiritual welfare so essential to the stability of
the entire community—does not make its appearance until
the end of the last tale. Although this tournament is presumably like the preceding ones, the narrative here is exclusively focused on the absurdity of the entire occasion. At
the outset Lancelot is nearly prevented from winning worship
because a young lady is inconsiderate enough mistakenly to
lodge an arrowhead in his buttock. This incident, humil-
iating as it is to Lancelot, amounts to a burlesque of chivalry:
it implies that worship cannot be worth much if it is thwarted
by such an obstacle. Lancelot's antisocial behavior in the
tournament seems entirely without point, and although Gareth and others save the situation, we see that the tournament
is meant to figure forth the irrevocable extent of the internal
confusion and the helplessness of Arthur's code in spite of
its revision. The final sentence emphasizes that the virtues
of the revised code are a response to and not an anticipation
of disorder: " 'And he that was curteyse, trew, and faythe-
full to hys frynde was *that tyme cherysshed'* " (790, italics
mine).

The conventional discourse on the seasons which opens
"The Knight of the Cart" forms another retrospective link
with the theme of instability in the Quest and looks for-
ward to the second thematic use of the seasonal metaphor as

an introduction to the final catastrophe in Tale VIII. Unlike the courtly use of seasonal reference in French poetry to describe a world "whose lovers sang within a paled green and sighed because the birds were gay and the ladies proud," Malory draws on the didactic English tradition to reintroduce the theme of mutability.[13] The passage stresses the hierarchy of love where the love of God is the only source of stability in other loves. By this spiritual standard we are to judge not only the instability of the Lancelot-Guenevere relationship, but also the failure of faith and love in the Round Table to "them that he promysed hys feythe unto" (791). The primacy of love for God can allow harmony in man's earthly loves because the proper love of one's lady founded on a love of God excludes "lycoures lustis" and thereby eliminates disloyalty to her husband. The sense of wasted potential enters the key sentence of this original passage: " 'And so in lyke wyse was used *such love* in kynge Arthurs dayes' " (791, italics mine.). Here we see the distinction between the fact that Arthurian society could, and at times did, use *such love* in the proper manner, and the certain implication that it also in other instances fell far short of the mark.

The passage about Guenevere who "whyle she lyved she was a trew lover, and therefor she had a good ende" (791) exemplifies this mixture of stable and unstable love which characterizes Arthurian society as a whole. Her adulterous relationship with Lancelot, as we have seen in the previous episodes, is unstable; but by virtue of its best aspects, her admiration of Lancelot's finest qualities and her faithfulness to him, she will be capable of spiritual stability and understanding in the end. The same development is true for the knights of the Round Table in the last tale. Here Malory's additions demonstrate that the reassertion of the best aspects of the Arthurian ideal combined with the spiritual understanding which should have defined it in the first place

13. Rosemond Tuve, *Seasons and Months: Studies in a Tradition of Middle English Poetry* (Paris, 1933), p. 181.

enable the members of the fellowship to make a good end. This entire introductory passage of Malory's argues for the proper hierarchy in love as a way of assuring stability. The political concerns of the book are directly related to this idea; that is, the establishment of a proper hierarchy in Arthurian society would have allowed the Round Table structure to perpetuate itself. But, as we have seen, Arthur's place in his society was defined ambiguously, as were the places of the other knights with respect to their affection for the king and for each other: we find that these relationships have been both dangerously idealized for their *caritas* and strongly underestimated for their quite natural fragility. The disruption of the Arthurian world which this opening passage of ''The Knight of the Cart'' reveals lies in the fact that the personal sphere of Arthurian society has supplanted the public sphere in the natural hierarchy of things, and thus there can be no *stabylité*.

We should note one more dimension to Malory's criticism of Arthur's fellowship before he turns to the tragedy of the last tale. The numerous echoes of the Grail quest in the earlier sections of Tale VII become doubly significant in ''The Healing of Sir Urry,'' which climaxes the tale. Here the entire Round Table, except Lancelot, is tested and proved unworthy. It is difficult to believe, as some critics seem to, that the parade of knights is a testament to the splendor of Arthur's court. Their failure to heal Sir Urry quite obviously indicates that Malory was interested in making the story reflect the spiritual sterility of the Round Table as a whole. Lancelot's success in this episode is simply an instance of grace designed as a reminder to him that each of his actions since the Quest has increased his distance from spiritual fulfillment. The spiritual implications of the episode necessarily run parallel to the suspense of the Lancelot-Guenevere theme: Lancelot's tears could be tears of relief that his adultery has not been discovered,[14] but they also indicate the realization

14. R. M. Lumiansky, ''The Tale of Lancelot and Guenevere,'' *Malory's Originality*, ed. R. M. Lumiansky (Baltimore, 1964), p. 231.

that his spiritual powers long neglected and abused are still available to him through grace. The fact that the Urry episode changes nothing for Lancelot spiritually suggests what we have seen over and over again—the inability of the Arthurian knight to make the individual spiritual step which will insure him and his fellows against disaster. The occasional sign of grace is an incongruous and painful event to the spiritually impotent.

Tale VIII

Malory's narrative moves very abruptly from the last test of the Round Table as a spiritual unit in Tale VII to the introduction of the tragic material of the *Morte Arthur*. The sudden transition here implies a cause and effect relationship between the loss of the structure's *spiritual* power and its ultimate defeat. This implication resembles the echoes of the Grail quest in the opening of Tale VII, which serve to tie the themes of those two tales together as well. Such emphasis on a cause and effect relationship between the events in the Arthurian story is not characteristic of Malory's sources. As Rosemond Tuve describes the tragedy of the king in the French romances, it is apparent that his decline has mysterious and unspecified origins which cannot be remedied in natural ways. There is no cause and effect in the French *Perlesvaus* and *Lancelot* because the king's fate simply stands for the ''deep sense of human inadequacy'' which is the theme of the romances.[15] Just as Malory inserted specific virtues and strengths to justify Arthur's election as king, he also avoids any interpretation which would suggest that the king's failure is only the result of some mysterious inadequacy fundamental to all human nature; the decline of Arthur has for Malory specific causes which relate to the political content of his book. Malory may have looked at the story without noting the symbolic meaning behind Arthur's loss of strength, seeing instead what his political milieu had

15. Rosemond Tuve, *Allegorical Imagery: Some Medieval Books and Their Posterity* (Princeton, 1966), p. 353.

prepared him to see—man's failure to perpetuate his institutions. The tragedy of the story for Malory does not lie in the
revelation of mortality or human inadequacy except insofar
as man fails to counteract these limitations with the permanence of his institutions. If this seems insufficient grounds
for the ''sense of loss'' necessary for ''tragic effect'' remember that the failure here is not simply the political one of
transient institutions, but the failure inherent in man's per-
sistent over-idealization of his own concepts and structures.
The real sense of desolation at the end of the *Morte* comes
from the fact that Malory has taken away not the glories of
Arthur, but our propensity to enjoy idealizing those glories
in our own interest—our wish to preserve the whole as an historical ideal of life. The parallel connection here between the
destructive weakness of the Arthurian knight cut loose from
the fellowship and the weakness of all later ideals which tie
themselves to the earlier model of Arthurian fellowship for
their survival is obvious and instructive. If we must talk
about tragic irony it can only be couched in the simultaneous
recognition of the patent glories of the Round Table and their
equally obvious unusability.

While Malory seems to have rejected implicitly one of the
commonplaces traditionally associated with Arthur's tragedy,
he has retained another because it has a political significance
which lies at the heart of his critique of the Round Table
structure. The relationship between the king and his fellowship in the French romances is binding to the extent that
neither the functions nor the obligations of either party exist
separately. Miss Tuve illuminates the force of this relationship by pointing out its sources: ''The identification of ruler
with realm and 'the sovereignty' was felt, even if the old belief had weakened in the intimate tie between the king's
health and the commonwealth's, an Arthurian common-
place.''[16] The only difference between what Miss Tuve describes as characteristic of the French romances, and Arthur's fellowship in *Le Morte Darthur* is that in the latter

16. *Ibid.*, p. 351.

the society is held responsible (its failure is not mysterious, but a consequence of specific mistakes) for the shortcomings of such an intimate and personal structure. To describe it in fifteenth-century political terms, the problem of Arthurian society is that the king's public and private persons are defined totally in terms of his fellowship, so that an attack on the king as a private individual necessitates catastrophe for the entire structure.

Tale VIII brings out the consequences of this identification of king and realm. Near the opening of the tale Aggravayne tells Arthur of Lancelot and Guenevere's adultery and in a sourceless passage says that he and Arthur's other nephews " 'wote that ye shulde be above Sir Lancelot, and ye ar the kynge that made hym knyght, and therefore we woll preve hit that he is a *traytoure to youre person'* " (919, Italics mine.). Lancelot has not only upset the natural hierarchy of things, but he has by sinning against the private person of the king (in having an affair with Guenevere) endangered the safety of Arthur's kingship as an office; this threat, of course, implies chaos for the entire realm. Here, then, is the final point at which Malory shows the relationship between the courtly love theme and the political ideal: in such a fragilely constructed society actions of a private nature have immense public consequences. Were Arthur's kingship independent of his fellowship and immortal as an office, the personal sins of his knights could not have had such consequences. On the other hand, the tragic aspect of the story is enhanced by Arthur's total dedication (both of his public and of his private person) to the society which he has created and holds as ideal, and Malory heightens this tension throughout the final episodes.

The extent to which Malory sought to employ the story of Arthur as a warning to his contemporaries is, of course, most pronounced in the last tale. He has traced the reciprocal loss of faith in the fellowship, and the fellowship's loss of energy and power since the end of Tale V. The process seems to occur in concentric circles beginning on the inside of the Round Table where the knights lose their sense of community and ignore their mutual obligations (in the Quest), and proceeding to the disillusionment of former friends (the holy man in Tale VII), and ending with the alienation of the community outside the fellowship. Earlier defined by its imposition of order in an unstable realm, the Round Table has become the very source of instability and the agent of disorder. The passage in which Malory describes in his own voice the disloyalty of the common people to Arthur is used to show that for initially defining itself by external successes the Round Table must take the consequences of the public's instability:

for than was the comyn voyce amonge them that with kynge Arthur was never othir lyff but warre and stryff, and with Sir Mordrede was grete joy and blysse. Thus was kynge Arthur depraved, and evyll seyde off; and many there were that kynge Arthur had brought up of nought, and gyffyn them londis, that myght nat than say hym a good worde.

Lo, ye all Englysshemen, se ye nat what a myschyff here was? For he that was the moste kynge and novelyst knyght of the worlde, and moste loved the felyshyp of noble knyghtes, and by hym they all were upholdyn, and yet myght nat thes Englysshemen holde them contente with hym. Lo thus was the olde custom and usayges of thys londe, and men say that we of thys londe have nat yet loste that custom. Alas! thys ys a greate defaughte of us Englysshemen, for there may no thynge us please no terme (861–62).

This passage is one of the best single examples of Malory's concern for the story as a warning to his times that government should be invulnerable to the passing fancy of the common people: the public has always been inconstant, but the government has not always allowed itself to fall prey to this inconstancy. The currents of fifteenth-century political thought supplied Malory with the leverage to expose the weakness of the Arthurian ideal.

We have seen how in the ''Quest'' the gradual dissolution of Round Table ties under conditions of stress resulted in the formation of new groups to comfort and protect the in-

dividual. By Tale VIII this process has had extreme consequences. Lancelot forms a following of knights with a
rallying speech (original with Malory) strikingly similar to
those used to describe Arthur's fellowship in the first four
tales: " 'Loke ye take no discomforte! For there ys no bondys
of knyghtes undir hevyn but we shall be able to greve them
as muche as they us, and therefore discomforte nat youreselff
by no maner. And we shall gadir togyder all that we love and
that lovyth us, and what that ye woll have done shall be
done. And therefore lat us take the wo and the joy togydir' "
(825). As the dialogue between Lancelot and his knights
proceeds (825–28, largely Malory's addition), we see that
the formation of splinter groups is a direct result of the
growing lack of trust in Arthur as king. When Lancelot is
advised that he will be able to return the queen to Arthur,
he likens himself to Tristram who was murdered by the
king after he returned Isolde to Mark's court. Only Bors reminds him " 'that kynge Arthur and kynge Marke were
never lkye of condycions' " (828).

But Lancelot's lack of faith in Arthur is not unfounded,
since in the interchange between Arthur and Gawain right
after the episode mentioned above Arthur acts not as king
and judge, but as a personal lord seeking revenge. Gawain's
advice to the king and the ensuing dialogue between them
(829–30) are greatly expanded by Malory. The passage
gives Arthur a significant portion of the responsibility for the
ultimate revenge of Gawain. At this point Gawain tries to
dissuade the king from sending Guenevere to the stake, but
Arthur is anxious for both Guenevere and Lancelot to suffer
shameful deaths. In the French, Guenevere's death sentence
is the baron's decision; but Malory assigns the responsibility
for the whole episode to Arthur, including the fateful presence of Gareth and Gaheris. Gawain explains to Arthur
that his two brothers will witness the scene only because Arthur has commanded them, and "they ar yonge and full unable to say you nay" (831, Malory's addition). The death
of Gawain's brothers and Gawain's revenge are thus very

largely the result of Arthur's unkingly behavior. In this passage he has totally ignored public good for the sake of private will, and Malory's changes and additions make this situation very clear.

In the light of Arthur's behavior here, it is not surprising that Gawain very easily persuades Arthur to abandon his office as judge and king and to honor instead the blood ties which will allow him to side with one of his knights against another. In this instance, again, the significance of the episode as it reflects on Arthur as a king is Malory's addition. Mr. Lumiansky has shown through source study that Malory has shifted the responsibility for Arthur's actions from Gawain to Arthur at this point.[17] Arthur's love for Gawain accounts for the fact that he opposed Lancelot despite his better instincts; Gawain has threatened Arthur not with the dissolution of the realm, but with the withdrawal of his love and support: " 'therefore, as ye woll have my servyse and my love . . . ' " (Malory's addition, 835). This interpretation by Malory is crucial, since Lancelot makes apparent later (838) that he and Arthur could be reconciled were it not for Arthur's personal loyalty to Gawain. Furthermore, in an original speech, Malory allows Lancelot to rebuke the king for the loss of honor Arthur has suffered as a result of this course of action: " 'My lorde, the kynge, for Goddis love, stynte thys stryff, *for ye gette here no worshyp* [italics added] and I wolde do myne utteraunce. But allwayes I forbeare you, and ye nor none off youres forberyth nat me . . . ' " (840).

The code of limited loyalty and personal ties begins to work as fate directing the actions of the king until at Gawain's request he makes the crucial decision to break the truce with Lancelot. He knows he has abdicated both the dignity and sanctity of his office by doing so, and it is now clear that the failure of individual responsibility and autonomy which his

17. R. M. Lumiansky, "Gawain's Miraculous Strength: Malory's Use of *le Morte Arthur* and *Mort Artu,*" *Etudes Anglaises*, X (1957), 97–108.

knights displayed in the Quest stemmed in part from the
weaknesses of Arthur himself. He cannot stand apart from
his personal ties in order to make the decisions which will
preserve his office, his fellowship, and his country. All of
Malory's additions and manipulations of Arthur's role in
Tales VII and VIII allow us to understand the causes of
his unreasoned acquiescence to Gawain's influence in this
crucial speech: " 'Now,' seyde kynge Arthur, 'wyte you
well, Sir Gawayne, I woll do as ye advyse me; and yet mesemyth,' seyde kynge Arthur, 'hys [Lancelot's] fayre proffers
were nat good to be reffused. But sytthen I am come so far
upon thys journey, I woll that ye gyff the damesell her an-
swere for I may nat speke to her for pité: for her profirs ben
so large' '' (835).

As the narrative progresses, Malory shows the Round
Table slowly redefining its code in more realistic political
terms. The experiences of Gawain, Arthur, Lancelot and the
surviving members of the Round Table show their belated
awareness that the failure in trust and love was ultimately
a failure to account for both the individual's responsibility
and his antisocial motives. Malory's final additions to the
story isolate the individual in order to emphasize that the
breaking of the fellowship is necessary to this discovery. The
substance of Gawain's letter to Lancelot (863) is Malory's
way of revealing that the conflict of loyalties was not inevitable, but indeed unnecessary. Gawain no longer defends
himself on the basis of a limited code of loyalty and revenge.
He at last recognizes his responsibility to a larger structure.
Malory's addition of this letter implies that if the Arthurian
society had actually been synonymous with Malory's fifteenth-
century political ideal at the outset, Gawain's acceptance of
individual responsibility and spiritual guidance would have
come in time to prevent catastrophe.

The Christian dimension of the tragedy, established by
the Grail quest, is not separate from the political inadequacies of the Round Table. It was Malory's genius to perceive the reciprocal relationship of political and spiritual

ends. From the beginning the implicit duty of the Round
Table (and by implication all good government) was the
creation of a social climate which would make the quest for
spiritual perfection possible. The Christian life is seen as
a pilgrimage towards salvation and the kingdom of God. The
journey or quest metaphor implies the necessity of movement
and growth, and these are made possible by amenable political and social conditions. Far from establishing such conditions, the Arthurian community has interfered with and
frozen spiritual movement.

The political failure is parallel to the spiritual collapse.
According to fifteenth-century political theory, Arthur's
tragedy is to have defined his fellowship so exclusively in
relation to his own worship, and conversely to have defined
himself and his office entirely as they relate to his fellowship,
making the destiny of his public person inseparable from
the destiny of the Round Table. His last moments reveal his
awareness of this double mistake. As his end approaches he
betrays his emptiness: " 'Jesu mercy!' seyde the kynge,
'where ar all my noble knyghtes becom? Alas, that ever I
shulde se thys doleful day! For now,' seyde kynge Arthur,
'*I* am com to myne ende' " (867). In this sourceless passage,
and in the greatly enlarged dialogue between Arthur and
Bedwer, Malory expands Arthur's tragedy to include the
king's gradual awareness that a society whose spiritual resources are vested in the personal magnetism of one man will
not be able to sustain his fellows: " 'Comforte thyselff,'
seyde the Kynge, 'and do as well as thou mayste, for in me
ys no truste for to truste in' " (871).

The incident with Bedwer is the final and most poignant
example of the king's impotence. Both Arthur and his society have lost their power to coerce individuals in a communal ideal: Bedwer, who in Tale II had been the special
object of Arthur's love and concern in a passage added by
Malory (161 bottom), now twice disobeys the king's final
request to throw Excaliber into the water. We must remember that in the alliterative *Morte* (Malory's source for Tale

II) Bedwer had been mortally wounded in the battle with
Lucius, but Malory preserved him in Tale II, perhaps with
this later episode in mind. Arthur finally realizes in the
speech to Bedwer that both Bedwer's failure in trust and
his desperate plea to the king for guidance are reciprocal
results of the society's inadequacy both as a communal and
as an individual ideal.

It is a measure of Malory's tragic sense and evidence of
his political concerns that Arthur's tragedy is directly attributable to his weaknesses as a king. At the point in the
French text where the king calls up the vicissitudes of fortune to explain his fall, Malory's Arthur simply declares all
"erthely joy ys gone" (863). Here, as in the scene with
Bedwer, the king understands that his loss of charisma is
responsible for the fragmentation of his fellowship. The
famous dream which occurs the night before the battle with
Mordred is drastically reduced in Malory's account. The
effect of this reduction is to change the interpretation of the
entire tragedy implicit in the French account of the dream.
The wheel of fortune in the *Mort Artu* is used as an explanation of the events leading up to Arthur's death, and Arthur's dream functions as a commentary on human frailty
and the inevitability of the king's decline. Malory's abbre-
viated and cryptic version does not mention the wheel by
name, and seems to work more as a description of Arthur's
emotional state than as an explanation of its causes. Here
as elsewhere Malory prefers to read the story as a tragedy
with well defined political causes than as a generalized tragedy in which the specific human event is dwarfed by fortune
and mortality.

Malory gives no credence to the myth of Arthur's return.
He records the various versions of Arthur's passing with the
impartial tone of the chronicler. To these he adds the only
personal statement he is willing to make on the mysterious
passing of the king: "rather I wolde sey *here in thys worlde
he chaunged hys lyff*" (873). We are to understand by this
that in death Arthur has shed the immortal part of his

twinned being which was inviolable in "thys worlde." This is the meaning Malory places on Arthur's passing. But the event carries with it another death since Arthur's fellowship is not immortal unless he is. Malory purposely extends his narrative beyond the ending in his source to record the death of the institution which is tied to both the mortal and the immortal persons of the king.

Like Arthur, Lancelot is led to at least a partial awareness of the necessary relationship between individual decision and the preservation of the community. When the code of a limited loyalty and fragmented attachments begins to work as fate in the final episodes, Lancelot realizes that he has allowed himself to be trapped by it: "'Alas,' seyde Sir Launcelot, 'I have no harte to fyghte ayenste my lorde Arthur, *for ever mesemyth I do not as me oughte to do.*'" (841, Italics mine.) Lancelot's end as a holy man points the way to a new fellowship based on spiritual fulfillment. Like the gesture of Galahad at the end of the "Quest," Lancelot's last request directs his fellows to cultivate the spiritual stability absent in the Arthurian code: "And anone as they had stablysshed theyr londes, for, the book saith, *so syr Launcelot commaunded them for to do or ever he passyd oute of thys world*, these foure knyghtes dyd many bataylles upon the myscreantes, or Turkes. And there they dyed upon a Good Fryday for Goddes sake." (883, italics mine.) Malory projects the story beyond its ending in his sources to include an account of the new fellowship of knights in the Holy Land. Here at last the author's concerns with permanence and stability are cast in a realizable form. But far from mitigating the tragic effect of the story, the additional passage shows us that this purely spiritual fellowship is necessarily emptied of the political promise which distinguished the Round Table ideal.

The seams of the Arthurian world are exposed in Malory's version as in no other. But paradoxically the tragedy is if anything more compelling for what we know about its origins. Were the story simply a fictional vehicle for rules of government, Arthur's passing would carry no greater emotional force than the final catastrophe of *Gorboduc*. But instead of reducing the moral complexity of the story's themes, Malory's political rendering of the legend enriches the story by allowing its paradoxes to emerge from the shroud of myth. The political idealism and political morality of the first four books show us why the Arthurian ideal deserves its reputation for true magnificence. And as the paradoxes of the story are then allowed full play we see that the order, civility, and ritual of this society of peers is only one half of a Janus-faced creature which also contains anarchy, fratricide, and the will to potential self-destruction. The politics of the story are only incidentally instructions for good government; primarily they are used to account for all aspects of the "mysterious" collapse of a perfect society. The tragic sense of Arthur's passing is preserved and even sharpened because politics for Malory is a very large category; it subsumes the history, the morality, and to a large degree, the religion of the story. Not only do we know that Arthur's passing is an irrevocable event, but we have learned that even the re-creation of Arthurian society as a cultural model or historical ideal must be at best an illusory and dangerous comfort.

Appendix

An Annotated Bibliography
of All Significant Malory Scholarship

I. EDITIONS

A. *The Major Editions**
1. 1485, William Caxton. *The noble and joyous hysterye of the grete conqueror and excellent Kyng, Kyng Arthur.*
   Two extant copies: the first and the only perfect copy is located in the Pierpont Morgan Library, New York; the second copy is in the John Rylands Library.
2. 1498, Wynkyn de Worde. *The booke of the noble Kyng, Kyng Arthur, sometyme Kynge of Englonde of his Noble actes and feates of armes of chyualrye, his noble knyghtes and table rounde and is devyded in to XXI. bookes.*
   Only extant copy of this edition is in the John Rylands Library and it is missing eleven pages. This edition is substantially the same as Caxton's except that Wynkyn de Worde has interpolated a passage that does not appear in Caxton.
3. 1529, Wynkyn de Worde. *The booke of the moost noble and worthy prince Kyng, Kyng Arthur, sometyme Kynge of grete Brytayne now called Englonde whiche treateth of his noble actes*

* For an excellent and complete account of this material, see the M.A. thesis by Thomas Rumble referred to in Section I. B.

[141]

and feates of armes and of chyualrye, of his noble knyghtes of
the table Rounde and this volume is devyded into XXI. bookes.
Only extant copy is in the British Museum. Differs somewhat
from Wynkyn's first edition. Title page, preface, and part of
the table of contents are gone.

4. 1557, Wyllyam Copland. *The Story of Kyng Arthur, and also*
of his noble and Valiante Knyghtes of the Rounde Table. Newly
imprynted and corrected. MCCCCCLVII. Imprynted at London
by Wyllyam Copland.

Of the three copies of Copland's edition in the British Museum, only one is perfect. Recent scholarly opinion points to
Wynkyn de Worde's edition as the source of Copland's text.

5. 1585, Thomas East. *The Story of Kynge Arthur, and also of*
his Knyghtes of the Rounde Table. Newly Imprynted and corrected between Paules wharfe and Baynardes Castell by Thomas
East.

Based directly on Copland.

6. 1634, W. Stansby. *The History of the Renowned Prince Arthur,*
King of Britaine. As also, all the Noble Acts and Heroicke
Deeds of his valiant Knights of the Round Table. 3 pts. London:
Printed by W. Stansby for Jacob Bloome, 1634.

Based on Thomas East's folio edition; Stansby divided his
edition into three parts and abandoned Caxton's division into
books. There are also some original interpolations and alterations in spelling.

7. 1816. *La Mort D'Arthur, The most ancient and famous historye*
of the Renowned Prince Arthur and the Knights of the Round
Table by Sir T. Malory. London, 1816.

A three-volume edition, the first of the Roman-type printings
and probably the first edition after Stansby's. Generally regarded as a remarkably poor job of editing.

8. 1816. *The History of the Renowned Prince Arthur, kyng of*
Britain with his life and death and all his glorious Battles, like-
wise the noble acts and heroic deeds of his valiant knights of
the Round table. London, 1816.

Another very poorly edited text in two volumes.

9. 1817. *The byrth, lyf and actes of Kyng Arthur; of his noble*
Knyghtes of the Rounde Table ther meruellous enquestes and
adventures thachyeuyng of the sanc greal, and in the end le
morte Darthur with the dolorous deth and departyng out of this
world of them al. With an introduction and notes by R. South-
ey. Printed from Caxton's edition, 1485. London, 1817.

A two-volume quarto edition which uses the imperfect John Ryland's copy of Caxton's edition for its text.

10. 1858. *La Morte d'Arthur. The History of King Arthur and of his Knights of the Round Table compiled by Sir Thomas Malory, Knt. edited from the text of the edition of 1634 with introduction and notes by Thomas Wright, Esq.* London, 1858.

Uses Stansby's edition and lets the emendations of that edition stand.

11. 1868. *Le Morte Darthur, Sir Thomas Malory's Book of King Arthur and of his Noble Knights of the Round Table. The Original Edition of Caxton Revised for Modern Use with an Introduction.* Globe Edition. London and New York, 1868.

Strachey's introduction to this edition indicates that it is meant for younger readers and consequently there are modernizations of obsolete words and spellings. The introduction also includes a history of the editions of Malory, an inquiry into the authorship and the matter of the book, and an essay on chivalry.

12. 1889. *Le Morte Darthur by Syr Thomas Malory, the original edition of William Caxton now reprinted and edited by H. Oskar Sommer, Ph.D.* Published by David Nutt in the Strand, 1889, 1890, 1891.

Three-volume edition. Volume I includes the text of *Le Morte Darthur* only. Volume II describes the editions and the language of the book and includes a list of proper names and a glossary. Volume III contains Sommer's study of Malory's sources and Andrew Lang's essay "Le Morte Darthur."

13. 1892. *The Noble and Joyous History of King Arthur by Sir Thomas Malory, edited by Ernest Rhys; Morte d'Arthur. The first nine books.* London: W. Scott, Ltd., Scott Library.

A modernized edition of Stansby's 1634 edition. The last twelve books were published in 1892 under the title *The Book of Marvellous Adventures and Other Books of the Morte Darthur.*

14. 1893. *The Birth, Life and Acts of King Arthur, of his Noble Knights of the Round Table, their Marvellous Enquests and Adventures, The Achieving of the San Greal, and in the end le Morte Darthur, with the Dolorous Death and Departing out of this World of them all. The text as Written by Sir Thomas Mallory and Imprinted by William Caxton at Westminster the year MCCCCLXXXV and now spelled in Modern Style. With an Introduction by Professor Rhys and Embellished with many Original Designs by Aubrey Beardsley.* 1893.

A two-volume edition. In 1906 it was reprinted for *Everyman's Library* and has been reissued in this and other forms several times. The introduction in Volume I of the first edition discusses Malory's birthplace and the Celtic elements of the Arthurian story.

15. 1897. *Le Morte D'Arthur by Sir Thomas Malory,* ed. Israel Gollancz. (The Temple Classics) London: Published by J. M. Dent and Company, Aldine House, 1897.

A four-volume edition based on Caxton with some modernized spellings. Volume IV contains bibliographical material and a glossary.

16. 1900. *Le Morte Darthur. Sir Thomas Malory's Book of King Arthur and of his Noble Knights of the Round Table.* (Library of English Classics). London: Macmillan and Company, 1900.

Two-volume edition by A. W. Pollard.

17. 1910, 1911. *Le Morte Darthur. The Book of King Arthur and of his Noble Knights of the Round Table. By Sir Thomas Malory, Knt.* 4 vols. London: Phillip Lee Warner, publisher to the Medici Society, Ltd., 1910–11.

A reprint of Pollard's 1900 edition with water colors by W. Russell Flint. Reissued in one volume without the water colors by University Books, 1961.

18. 1933. *The Noble and Joyous Boke entytled Le Morte Darthur.* 2 vols. Oxford: Oxford University Press, 1933.

Blackwell's reprint of the 1498 edition.

19. 1947. *The Works of Sir Thomas Malory,* ed. Eugene Vinaver. 3 vols. Oxford: Clarendon Press, 1947.

This edition is based on the fifteenth century manuscript of the *Morte Darthur* discovered in Winchester College Library by W. F. Oakeshott in 1934. The introduction in Volume I and the commentary and notes in Volume III set forth the theory that Malory wrote several independent romances rather than a single unified book. The notes in Volume III also compare Malory's version with his supposed sources. Other aids include a bibliography of editions and criticism, an index and a glossary.

20. 1954. *The Works of Sir Thomas Malory.* (Oxford Standard Authors) New York: Oxford University Press, 1954.

A one-volume reprint of Vinaver's 1947 edition with an introduction.

21. 1955. *The Tale of the Death of King Arthur,* ed. Eugene Vinaver. Oxford: Oxford University Press, 1955.

The last of the *Works,* re-edited with additional introduction, notes and corrections.

22. 1956. *King Arthur and His Knights: Selections From the Works of Sir Thomas Malory.* (Riverside Editions, B8.) Boston: Houghton Mifflin Co., 1956.

23. 1967. *The Works of Sir Thomas Malory,* ed. Eugene Vinaver. 2d ed. 3 vols. Oxford: Clarendon Press, 1967.

Contains revisions of critical apparatus in the 1947 edition as well as some additions to the *Commentary.* More source material is brought to bear on Tale I, but Vinaver's opinions on the matter of unity and originality remain unchanged. The bibliography is brought up to date.

B. *Commentary on Editors, Editions and Manuscripts*

1. Anonymous. "Malory's Morte D'Arthur," *Bulletin John Rylands Lib.,* XVIII (1934), 15.

   Comment on Blackwell's reprint of 1498 edition.

2. Anonymous. "Malory's Mort d'Arthur," *Bulletin John Rylands Lib.,* XIX (1935), 19–21.

   Comment on manuscript at Winchester College.

3. Anonymous. "The Malory Enigma," *London Times Literary Supplement,* March 16, 1946, p. 127.

4. Anonymous. "The Morte Darthur," *London Times Literary Supplement,* June 7, 1947, pp. 273–74.

   Leading article on Vinaver's edition of the Winchester manuscript. The author finds that Vinaver's separation of Malory's work into eight separate romances "impoverishes" one's reading of the *Morte.*

5. Bühler, C. F. "Two Caxton Problems," *Library,* 4th Series, XX (1940), 266–71.

   Two arguments showing that Caxton's *Le Morte Darthur* was printed as a folio rather than as a quarto volume.

6. Kenyon, F. G. "Morte Darthur," *London Times Literary Supplement,* June 7, 1947, p. 281.

   Letter to editor.

7. Markland, Murray F. "The Role of William Caxton," *Research Studies* (Washington State University, Pullman), XXVIII (1960), 47–60.

   Concerned primarily with Caxton's aims, audience and taste. Minimizes "revolutionary" effects of printing in fifteenth-century England. Finds Caxton's taste antiquarian and his intentions those of an afficionado with a wealthy audience to please.

8. Oakeshott, W. F. *Times*, 26 June and 25 August, 1934.

On the newly discovered Winchester manuscript of *Le Morte Darthur*.

9. ———. "The Text of Malory," *London Times Literary Supplement*, September 27, 1934, p. 650.

Concerns the Winchester manuscript.

10. ———. "The Finding of the Manuscript," in *Essays on Malory*, ed. J. A. W. Bennett. Oxford, 1963. Pp. 1–6.

Oakeshott's account of his discovery of the Winchester Manuscript.

11. Richards, Gertrude R. B. "An Early Edition of the 'Morte d'Arthur,'" *More Books* (January, 1946), pp. 18–20.

Summarizes Kittredge's biographical information. A description of Thomas East's edition of Malory which dates around 1582.

12. Rumble, Thomas C. "A Survey of the Editions and Criticism of Sir Thomas Malory's Morte D'Arthur." Master's thesis, Tulane University, 1950.

An excellent annotated listing describing each major edition.

13. Shaw, Sally. "Caxton and Malory," in *Essays on Malory*, ed. J. A. W. Bennett. Oxford, 1963. Pp. 114–45.

A comparison of Caxton's edition with the Winchester manuscript showing that the latter is undoubtedly closer to what Malory wrote. The major part of the essay demonstrates that Caxton's skill as a stylist and editor makes his edition superior to Winchester manuscript.

14. Vinaver, E. "Malory's Morte D'Arthur," *John Rylands Lib. Bulletin*, XIX (1935), 438–57.

Diagrams the relationship between Caxton's edition and the Winchester manuscript by using evidence from Malory's sources. Reconstructs the lost source common to both Caxton and Winchester. Points out significant differences in theme and emphasis between Caxton and Winchester.

15. Vinaver, E. "Principles of Textual Emendation," in *Studies . . . presented to Professor Mildred K. Pope*. Manchester, 1939. Pp. 350–69.

16. ———. "A Note on the Earliest Printed Texts of Malory's Morte Darthur," *Bulletin John Rylands Lib.*, XXIII (1939), 102–6.

A short discussion of the variants between the two copies

of Caxton's edition of *Le Morte Darthur*. Some technical information on early methods of printing. Concludes that the Rylands copy preserves Caxton's unrevised text in its original form.

17. ———. "Le Manuscrit de Winchester," *Bulletin Bibliographique de la Société Internationale Arthurienne*, III (1951), 75–82.

Finds that the Winchester manuscript presents the "true Malory," and declares that Caxton's edition constantly interposes a third person, the editor, between Malory and the reader. Goes through early critical opinions of the structure of *Le Morte Darthur* and concludes that the unity which critics have found there never existed. Points out the contrast between Caxton and Malory and establishes it as the kind of contrast which exists between the novel of the Middle Ages and the modern novel. Caxton's editorial concerns were for an external order which he could impose upon the work.

II. LANGUAGE AND STYLE

1. Baldwin, Charles S. *The Inflections and Syntax of the Morte Darthur*, Boston, 1894.

2. ———. "The Verb in the *Morte d'Arthur*," *Modern Language Notes*, X, no. 2 (1895), 46–47.

This article explains certain of the classifications of Malory's verbs which the author included in his book *The Inflections and Syntax of the Morte Darthur* (Boston, 1894).

3. Chambers, R. W. "English Prose Alfred to More," *Early English Text Society*, No. 186 (1932).

Concludes that *Le Morte Darthur* is not in the "general line of progress" of English prose style. Treats Malory's style as if it were consciously archaic and therefore appropriate to his "antique" subject matter.

4. Dekker, A. *Some Facts Concerning the Syntax of Malory's Morte Darthur*. Amsterdam, 1932.

5. Field, P. J. C. "Description and Narration in Malory," *Speculum*, 43 (1968), 476–86.

An interesting study of Malory's style as an indicator of the reader and the writer's degree of involvement in the action. All of Malory's stylistic techniques work to unify the narrative and to augment realism.

6. Goodman, John Stuart. "The Syntax of the Verb 'To Be' in Malory's Prose." Ph.D. dissertation, University of Michigan, 1962.

7. Hempl, George, "The Verb in the 'Morte D'Arthur,'" *Modern Language Notes*, IX, no. 8 (1894), 240–41.

Finds that Baldwin's treatise *The Inflections and Syntax of the Morte d'Arthur* reveals some oversights. Hempl adds to Baldwin's lists of verbs.

8. Hungerford, Harold Roe, Jr. "Comparative Constructions in the Work of Sir Thomas Malory: A Synchronic Study," *Dissertation Abstracts*, 24 (1963), 5399 (California).

Investigates three sets of comparative constructions: those with *as . . . as, so . . . as,* and *such . . . as*; those with *more . . . than* and *-er . . . than*; those with *so . . . that* and *such . . . that.*

9. Martin, Lynn S. "Sir Thomas Malory's Vocabulary in 'The Tale of Arthur and Lucius,' 'The Tale of Sir Gareth', and 'The Tale of the Sank-Greal': A Comparative Study," *Dissertation Abstracts* 27 (1966), 1376A (Pennsylvania).

10. Phillips, K. C. "Contamination in Late Middle English," *Englische Studien*, XXXV (1954), 17–20.

Includes examples from Malory.

11. Rioux, Robert N. "Sir Thomas Malory, Createur Verbal," *Etudes Anglaises*, XII (1959), 193–97.

12. Sandved, Arthur Olav. "A Note on the Language of Caxton's Malory and That of the Winchester MS," *English Studies*, XL (1959), 113–14.

Compares the language of the two versions in the "Tale of Lancelot" and in the "Tale of Gareth." Assumes a common source for both versions which probably represented a corrected version of Malory's text.

13. Simko, Ján. *Word Order in the Winchester Manuscript and in William Caxton's Edition of Thomas Malory's Morte Darthur —A Comparison.* Halle, 1957.

Concentrates on Tale II and compares the two versions of *Le Morte Darthur* with the alliterative *Morte Arthure*. Malory attempted to make the language of his source much simpler and more straightforward. Caxton's tendency is to regularize Malory's word order and to create for the tale something of a "literary language."

14. Smith, G. Gregory. *The Transition Period.* Edinburgh, 1900.

Brief discussion of Malory's prose style with a comparison of Malory to some of his contemporaries.

III. GENERAL STUDIES OF MALORY

1. Adams, Robert P. "Bold Bawdry and Open Manslaughter: The

English New Humanist Attack on Medieval Romance," *Huntington Library Quarterly*, XXIII (1959), 33–48.

An attempt to understand the New Humanist attacks on medieval romance (especially the attacks of More, Erasmus, and Vives) as more moderate and sensible than recent critics have admitted. According to Adams, the New Humanists would not accept the identification of romance and history which Caxton made in his preface to the 1485 edition of *Le Morte Darthur*.

2. Arthos, John. *On the Poetry of Spenser and the Form of the Romances.* London, 1959.

Briefly explores Malory's handling of the adventures and events of the romance to throw light on Spenser's use of the genre. He notes that the deliberately vague atmosphere surrounding both actions and emotions in *Le Morte Darthur* and in Spenser is part of the authors' central conception of the isolated and potentially self-sufficient individual's journey through an uncharted world.

3. Atabay, Ercüment. "Büyuk Ingiliz Destanlari [The Great English Epics], *Morte D'Arthur*," *Yenitürk*, IX (1941), 706–9.

4. Aurner, N. S. "Sir Thomas Malory-Historian?" *Publications of the Modern Language Association*, XLVIII (1933), 362–91.

An important article which characterizes much of the Malory scholarship of this century. Objects to the mingling of chronicle and romance, the lengthy Tristram section, the departures from the versions of some stories as they are found in the Vulgate cycle. Malory's method of composition is explained in autobiographical terms: "He would translate not merely into his own language but into his own life and times as well." Miss Aurner also works out the parallels between the three stages of Arthur's career and the careers and personalities of Henry IV, Henry V, and Henry VI.

5. Baker, Sister I. *The King's Household in the Arthurian Court From Geoffrey of Monmouth to Malory.* Washington, D.C., 1937.

6. Bennett, J. A. W., ed. *Essays on Malory.* Oxford, 1963.

Contents: W. F. Oakeshott, "The Finding of the Manuscript."
C. S. Lewis, "The English Prose *Morte*."
E. Vinaver, "On Art and Nature: A Letter to C. S. Lewis."
D. S. Brewer, " 'The Hoole Book.' "
P. E. Tucker, "Chivalry in the *Morte*."
F. Whitehead, "Lancelot's Penance."
Sally Shaw, "Caxton and Malory."

These essays were compiled as a response to Vinaver's 1947 edition of the Winchester manuscript. The editor insists that the "volume is not a collaborative effort, and no attempt has been made to tone down differences." Descriptions of individual essays appear in their appropriate headings.

7. Bennett, J. W. "Britain Among the Fortunate Isles," *Studies in Philology*, LIII (1956), 114–40.

Allusions to Malory and Ariosto, and discussion of Spenser's *Faerie Queene* are used to explore the ancient notion that England was one of the Fortunate Isles, or Islands of the Blest.

8. Benson, Larry D. "Le Morte Darthur," in *Critical Approaches to Six Major English Works*, ed. R. M. Lumiansky. Philadelphia, 1968.

Provides an excellent summary of trends in Malory scholarship and then proposes that Malory can be best appreciated if he is read as the unique creator of a *fifteenth-century English* romance, and not as an antiquarian or a precocious novelist.

9. Bradbrook, Muriel C. *Sir Thomas Malory.* (Writers and Their Work, No. 95) London, New York, Toronto, 1958.

Six short chapters: The Knight Prisoner; Knightly Romance; The English Round Table; Malory and the Heroic Tradition; Tragic Themes in Malory; Day of Destiny. A good introduction to Malory which emphasizes Malory's concentration on the social aspects of the Arthurian story.

10. Brewer, D. S. "Form in the *Morte Darthur*," *Medium Aevum*, XXI (1952), 14–24.

Examines Malory's narrative technique to demonstrate the unity of the whole book. As evidence for unity Brewer notes all linking passages and outlines the three major movements of the book to show that the last two are each dependent upon the movement which precedes them.

11. ———. " 'The hoole book,' " in *Essays on Malory*, ed. J. A. W. Bennett. Oxford, 1963. Pp. 41–63.

Suggests the substitution of the word *cohesion* for *unity* in discussing the connectedness of Malory's tales. Points out that Malory's handling of the story increases its historical nature and consequently contributes to the reader's sense of cohesion. Brewer traces all the chronological references in the book and concludes that the time scheme is well designed for the presentation of tragedy and therefore the tales cannot be read in any order other than the one we have.

12. Catalan, Diego. *De Alphonso X al Conde de Barcelos. Cuatro Estudios. Sobre el nacimiento de la historiografía romance en*

Castilla y Portugal. Madrid: Universidad de Madrid y Editorial Gredos, 1962.

Mentions Malory as a possible source for the battle of Camlan in Pedro de Barcelos' *Libro das Linhagens.*

13. Chambers, E. K. *Sir Thomas Wyatt and Some Collected Studies.* London, 1933.

Reprints the essay "Sir Thomas Malory" first published in English Association Pamphlet 51, 1922. Notes the inconsistencies of characterization and the incoherent structural plan of *Le Morte Darthur.* Sees Malory as an antiquarian presenting to his countrymen "the ideal of a better England."

14. Chambers, E. K. *English Literature at the Close of the Middle Ages.* Oxford, 1945.

Chambers' chapter on Malory appeared before Vinaver's edition of the Winchester manuscript, although he was aware of the manuscript's existence. Chambers maintains that the eight tales are to be read as chapters in a continuous narrative. He does, however, agree with Vinaver that Malory was a fifteenth-century gentleman concerned with revitalizing the moral fibre of English society by presenting the model of a chivalric society. He shows a certain amount of skepticism concerning the traditional biographical material connected with Malory.

15. Cooksey, C. F. "The Morte d'Arthur," *Nineteenth Century* (June, 1924), pp. 852–59.

A lyrical essay in praise of a book which "arouses all the higher emotions of mankind." There is also a subsidiary thesis which holds that "the basic element in the *Morte d'Arthur* is the Celtic story" which records the arrival of the apostolic missionaries to the shores of England. King Arthur is therefore to be identified with King Caradoc.

16. Davies, R. T. "Quelques Aspects Sociaux de l'oeuvre de Malory, en particulier sa conception de l'amour." Abstract in *Bulletin Bibliographique de la Société Internationale Arthurienne,* III (1951), 103.

This abstract presents a concise statement of the material present in Davies' article "Malory's 'Vertuouse Love,' " *Studies in Philology,* LIII.

17. ————. "Malory's Lancelot and the Noble Way of the World," *Review of English Studies* N.S., VI (1955), 356–64.

The "noble way" referred to in the article's title is the way of secular chivalry. The article proceeds from a definition of Malory's ideal to an examination of its limitations as a realistic guide to behavior. Davies believes that the clash of loyalties which the "noble way" produces is Malory's most original contribution to the story.

18. ———. "Malory's 'Vertuouse Love,'" *Studies in Philology,* LIII (1956), 459–69.

"Inconsistencies" in Malory's treatment of love stem from Malory's distinction between faithful love and promiscuous love. Lancelot and Guenevere are virtuous lovers because they are loyal to each other in love. Explains the limits of Malory's approval of such love.

19. ———. "The Worshipful Way in Malory," in *Patterns of Love and Courtesy: Essays in Memory of C. S. Lewis,* ed. John D. Lawlor. London, 1966. Pp. 157–77.

Elaborates on earlier articles dealing with Malory's views about love. He sees Malory's position as something of an attempt to reconcile romantic love and Christianity.

20. Dubois, Marguerite-Mary. *Le Roman d'Arthur et ses chevaliers de la Table Ronde.* 1948.

21. Dundes, Alan. "The Father, the Son, and the Holy Grail," *Literature and Psychology,* XII (1962), 101–12.

An allegorical reading of the Arthurian story which stems from the work of Otto Rank. Malory's book is cited as an example of the "son-hero" pattern with full Oedipal overtones.

22. Effland, Evelyn Leigh. "Plot, Character, Theme: A Critical Study of Malory's *Works,*" *Dissertation Abstracts,* XXVI (1965), 354 (Denver).

Interprets theme and characters symbolically and analyzes Malory's technical mastery of plot. Sees the *Works* as Malory's vision of a near-perfect earthly civilization.

23. Erskine, John. "Malory's Le Morte d'Arthur," *The Delight of Great Books.* Indianapolis, 1928. Pp. 53–71.

An armchair reading of Malory. Erskine finds that Malory has created a world with no subtleties in it. The appeal of his book lies in the "dramatic vigor" with which incidents are related and in the reader's recognition of characters and stories which Malory's successors took from him.

24. Ferguson, Arthur B. *The Indian Summer of English Chivalry: Studies in the Decline and Transformation of Chivalric Idealism.* Durham, N. C., 1960.

Discusses Malory as a moralist who employed chivalry as a virtuous example for his countrymen to follow. Malory's concept of chivalry is defined in very simple terms as "the practical function of a well established order." Ferguson makes a sharp distinction between Malory's ideal of knighthood and the chivalry of courtoisie or religious mysticism both of which belong to an earlier age. (Malory, pp. 42–58; Arthurian legend and literature, pp. 98–103.)

25. Field, P. J. C. "Description and Narration in Malory," *Speculum*, XLIII (July, 1968), 476–86.
Concentrates primarily upon the descriptive and narrative methods of the Balin story. Finds Malory's style emotionally compelling even though actual visual description is rarely employed. Notes how Malory's syntax gives the appearance that "flat truth" is being conveyed without the intervention of the author. Close comparison with the narrative method of the Balin story in Malory's source reveals the reasons behind Malory's superior version.

26. Fiester, Ben F. "The Function of the Supernatural in Malory's *Morte Darthur*," *Dissertation Abstracts*, 28 (1967), 4124A–25A (Pennsylvania State).

27. Fox, Ralph. *The Novel and the People*. London, 1937.
Views Malory as "the first great escapist, a man seeking refuge from a fearful present in an idealized past."

28. Goldman, Marcus Selden. "Sir Philip Sidney and the Arcadia," *University of Illinois Studies in Language and Literature*. Urbana, 1935.
Sidney's indebtedness to Malory.

29. Hampsten, Elizabeth. "A Reading of Sir Thomas Malory's *Morte Arthur*," *North Dakota Quarterly*, 35 (1967), 29–37.

30. Hobar, Donald. "The Oral Tradition in Malory's *Morte Darthur*," *Dissertation Abstracts*, 28 (1967) 3639A (Pittsburgh).

31. Houghton, R. E. C. "Letter of Matthew Arnold," *London Times Literary Supplement*, May 19, 1932, p. 368.
On Arnold's Tristram and Iseult with editorial comment on Malory.

32. Kennedy, Edward D. "King Arthur and King Mark: Aspects of Kinship in Malory's Morte Darthur," *Dissertation Abstracts*, 28 (1967), 3145A–46A (Illinois).

33. Lang, Andrew. "Le Morte Darthur," in *Le Morte Darthur by Sir Thomas Malory*, ed. H. O. Sommer, III, 1891, XIII–XXV.
A brief introduction to Sommer's edition. Characterizes the appeal of Malory's language and tone as that of "childlike simplicity." Includes a comparison of Homer and Malory and one between Malory's story of Arthur and the Arthurian literature of his successors.

34. Lascelles, Mary. "Sir Dagonet in Arthur's Show," *Shakespeare Jahrbuch*, XCVI (1960), 145–54.
Speculates on Shakespeare's knowledge of Malory from his reference to Sir Dagonet in *2 Henry IV* (III, ii) and from

certain parallels between Malory's Sir Dinaden and Shakespeare's Falstaff.

35. Levy, G. R. *The Sword From the Rock*. London, 1953.

A brief consideration of *Le Morte Darthur* as an epic comparable to the works of Homer and the *Chanson de Roland*.

36. Lewis, C. S. "The English Prose *Morte*," in *Essays on Malory*, ed. J. A. W. Bennett. Oxford, 1963. Pp. 7–28.

It is Lewis' intention to settle some major issues in Malory studies by considering the following five problems: the apparent paradox of Malory's villainous life and his moral book; the use of marvellous; the narrative method of *entrelacement*; the importance of the religious material; the author's intention to write one book or several separate works. Lewis' conclusions on these matters are intended as a corrective for Vinaver's opinions.

37. Loudon, Katherine Mary. *Two Mystic Poets and Other Essays*. Oxford, 1922.

King Arthur in Malory and Tennyson.

38. Lumiansky, R. M., ed. *Malory's Originality: A Critical Study of Le Morte Darthur*. Baltimore, 1964.

R. M. Lumiansky, "Introduction," pp. 1–7; Thomas L. Wright, " 'The Tale of King Arthur': Beginnings and Foreshadowings," 9–66; Mary E. Dichmann, " 'The Tale of King Arthur and the Emperor Lucius': The Rise of Lancelot," 67–90; R. M. Lumiansky, " 'The Tale of Lancelot': Prelude to Adultery," 91–98; Wilfred L. Guerin, " 'The Tale of Gareth': The Chivalric Flowering," 99–117; Thomas C. Rumble, " 'The Tale of Tristram': Development by Analogy," 118–83; Charles Moorman, " 'The Tale of Sankgreall': Human Frailty," 184–204; R. M. Lumiansky, " 'The Tale of Lancelot and Guenevere': Suspense," 205–32; Wilfred L. Guerin, " 'The Tale of the Death of Arthur': Catastrophe and Resolution," 233–74.

The introduction explains that the essays are unified in approaching *Le Morte Darthur* through a comparison of it with its sources. This kind of source study is designed to prepare the way for studies of theme and structure. The individual essays are discussed under their appropriate headings.

39. Lumiansky, R. M. "The Question of Unity in Malory's *Morte Darthur*," *Tulane Studies in English*, V (1955), 29–39.

Takes issue with Vinaver's point that since the time sequence of Malory's narrative is not strictly chronological the book it not unified. Shows that Malory makes use of an internal time scheme which occasionally relies on "retrospective narrative" when strict chronology is abandoned; this explains the relationship between Tales III and IV and between Tales IV and V. See D. S. Brewer's review in *Medium Aevum*, XXV, no. 1 (1956), 22–26.

40. Miko, Stephen J. "Malory and the Chivalric Order," *Medium Aevum*, XXXV (1966), 211–30.

Chivalric order in Malory's book is based on family ties, "blood." Tragedy in the book results from conflict of relatives.

41. Moorman, Charles. "Courtly Love in Malory," *English Literary History*, XXVII (1960), 163–76.

Insists that Malory knew what he was doing with courtly love, and that he purposely set out to exploit the paradoxical nature of courtly love which he found in his sources. Finds that virtuous love is constantly set apart from courtly love and the tragic consequences which proceed from it.

42. ———. "Internal Chronology in Malory's *Morte Darthur*," *Journal of English and Germanic Philology*, LX (1961), 240–49.

An explanation of the puzzling chronological relation of Books II, III, IV, and the first sections of V. With the aid of a graph and some discussion of the book's major themes, Moorman concludes that "Malory presents his tales in their natural thematic order and suggests by implication their proper chronological arrangement.

43. Moorman, Charles. "Lot and Pellinore: The Failure of Loyalty in Malory's 'Morte Darthur,'" *Mediaeval Studies* (Toronto), XXV (1963), 83–92.

Isolates the Lot-Pellinore feud as one of three plot devices which unify *Le Morte Darthur*. Describes the new chivalry of Arthurian society and the forces which undermine it.

43. ———. *The Book of Kyng Arthur: The Unity of Malory's Morte Darthur*. Lexington, 1965.

Moorman uses thematic analysis of Malory's book to demonstrate its unity. *Le Morte Darthur* was designed to encompass the "rise, flowering, and downfall of a well-nigh perfect civilization." For his purposes Malory has singled out three themes from his sources and has woven his narrative around them. Moorman examines what he calls the "Failure in Love," the "Failure in Religion," and "the Failure in Chivalry" as these themes appear in the narrative.

44. ———. "Malory's Tragic Knights," *Mediaeval Studies* (Toronto), XXVII (1965), 117–27.

A very significant article on the literary history of knight errantry. Exposes the central paradox of traditional views on Malory's chivalry by asking why Malory concluded by damning chivalry if, as critics say, he was so intent upon reviving its values for his own day.

45. ———. *A Knyght There Was: The Evolution of the Knight in Literature.* Lexington, 1967.

46. Muecke, D. C. "Some Notes on Vinaver's Malory," *Modern Language Notes*, LXX (1955), 325–28.

Points to five or six of Vinaver's comments on the text which need revising. Vinaver's errors in judgment seem to stem here from his scepticism about Malory's originality and/or competence as a literary artist.

47. Muir, Lynette R. "A Detail in Milton's Description of Sin," *Notes and Queries*, N.S., 111 (1956), 100–101.

The detail referred to may have been suggested by Malory's Questing Beast.

48. Read, Herbert. *The Nature of Literature.* New York, 1956.

Notes ways in which Malory's merit has been misrepresented either by sentimental readers or by what he calls "anti-romantic" critics.

49. Reiss, Edmund. *Sir Thomas Malory.* New York, 1966.

Not concerned with sources and structure as much as with the book's function as a work of literary art. Views Malory as a moralist with a desire to "oversimplify or to turn away from the present." Reiss does a thematic investigation of the book episode by episode using a great deal of St. Augustine to support his views about Malory's intentions.

50. Rumble, Thomas C. "The First *Explicit* in Malory's *Morte Darthur*," *Modern Language Notes*, LXXI (1956), 564–66.

Questions Vinaver's reading of Malory's first Explicit, noting that the paragraphing of the *Explicit* is Vinaver's and not indicated in the Winchester manuscript. Thinks the first three lines are actually part of the tale and that the *explicit* itself consists of only the last six lines. Believes that the phrase "this book endyth" refers to Malory's source and not to his own tale. The explicit therefore signifies Malory's intention to begin following another source.

51. ———. "Malory's *Works* and Vinaver's Comments: Some Inconsistencies Resolved," *Journal of English and Germanic Philology*, LIX (1960), 59–69.

Finds Vinaver guilty of attributing inconsistencies to Malory which do not exist. Most of Vinaver's errors are, according to Rumble, matters of misinterpretation of the text. Rumble argues for a greater degree of skill in Malory's book than Vinaver will admit, and he emphasizes the importance of understanding the technique of compression which Malory uses in translating a source.

52. Schlauch, Margaret. *Antecedents of the English Novel 1400–1600*. London, 1963.

    Interested in Malory's contribution to the direction of English fiction. Notes his reliance on motivation instead of magic and the supernatural, and his preference for concentrating upon the human involvements which lay hidden in his sources.

53. Schofield, W. H. *Chivalry in English Literature: Chaucer, Malory, Spenser and Shakespeare*. Cambridge, 1912.

    Finds *Le Morte Darthur* exclusively aristocratic in tone and sentiment. Credits Malory with making Arthurian figures national heroes by his intensification of the idealism and patriotism of the story. Reads a good deal of political allegory into the book.

54. Schutt, J. H. "A Guide to English Studies," *English Studies*, XII (1930), 98–108.

    Includes remarks on Malory.

55. Simko, Ján. "Thomas Malory's Creed" in *Studies in Language and Literature in Honor of Margaret Schlauch*. Warsaw, 1966. Pp. 437–44.

    Argues the question of Malory's point of view in handling his sources and concludes that although Malory made the story of his French sources more realistic by giving it a political purpose, he was basically an escapist writer. Simko insists that Malory looked for a reinstatement of an improved chivalry to solve the problems which beset Arthur's society and his own.

56. Snell, F. J. *The Age of Transition, 1400–1580*, Vol. II: *The Dramatists and the Prose Writers*. London, 1905.

    Brief summary of early biographical investigations of Malory. Praises Malory for creative style and rapidity of narrative. Condemns the author for his lack of respect for "the sanctity of marriage."

57. Stewart, G. R. "English Geography in Malory's Morte D'Arthur," *Modern Language Review*, XXX (1935), 204–9.

    Shows Malory's interest in localizing the scene of his narrative and his desire to make the story more historical and less mythical.

58. Tillyard, E. M. W. "Malory Re-edited," *The Cambridge Review*, October 25, 1947, pp. 54ff.

    A critique of Vinaver's opinion that Malory reduced the idealism of his French sources to a homely realism.

59. Thearle, Beatrice June. "Malory in the Nineteenth Century," *Dissertation Abstracts*, XIX (1958–59), 133 (University of Maryland).

60. Thornton, Sister M. M. *Malory's Morte Darthure as a Christian Epic.* Urbana, Ill., 1936.

61. Tucker, P. E. "Chivalry in the *Morte*," in *Essays on Malory*, ed. J. A. W. Bennett. Oxford, 1963. Pp. 64–103.

A study of the ideal of chivalry which Malory substituted for that found in his French sources. Tucker sees chivalry as the most important single element in the book and suggests that it was the reason for Malory's initial interest in the Arthurian story. Malory's chivalry is unique for its unqualified virtues as a guide to conduct. Tucker insists that Malory is only capable of criticizing the chivalric ideal when he explores its connection with courtly love.

62. Vinaver, E. *Sir Thomas Malory.* Oxford, 1929.

Vinaver's major statement about Malory prior to the discovery of the Winchester manuscript. Contains speculation on Malory's life and a study of Caxton and his edition as well as chapters on the genesis of Arthurian romance and courtly love; Malory's narrative technique; chivalry; romance and realism; Camelot and Corbenil; Malory's translations and his style. There is also an appendix with biographical material, a source study of the *Queste*, and a bibliography.

63. ———. "Sir Thomas Malory," *Arthurian Literature in the Middle Ages.* Oxford, 1959. Pp. 541–52.

Vinaver reiterates his opinion that Malory's "works" reveal unity of manner and style, but not of design. Vinaver reads the final tale as a self-contained tragedy motivated by a "clash of loyalties" within the society. Does not credit Malory with any original compositions. Makes some useful comments on the kinds of style which Malory employs.

64. ———. "On Art and Nature," in *Essays on Malory*, ed. J. A. W. Bennett. Oxford, 1963. Pp. 29–40.

This is Vinaver's answer to Lewis' article which appears in the same book. Vinaver refutes Lewis' objections and demonstrates that he has not changed his mind on any of the five major issues which Lewis raised.

65. ——— *Form and Meaning in Medieval Romance.* Presidential Address of the Modern Humanities Research Association, 1966. Published by the MHRA.

Although it is not directly concerned with Malory, this piece illuminates much about Vinaver's method of reading *Le Morte Darthur.*

66. ———. "Epic and Tragic Patterns in Malory," in *Friendship's Garland: Essays Presented to Mario Praz on His Seventieth*

Birthday, ed. Vittorio Gabrieli. 2 vols. Rome, 1966. Vol. 1, pp. 81–85.

A brief account of a radio broadcast by Mario Praz in which he commented on the modernity of Malory's narrative style.

67. Vincent, Ruby Ruth. "A Comparison of Malory's *Morte Darthur* and Tennyson's *Idylls of the King*," Master's thesis, University of Oklahoma, 1939. (Abstract in University of Oklahoma Bull., No. 760, p. 119.)

68. Walker, R. A. "Le Morte Darthur," *London Times Literary Supplement*, March 31, 1945, p. 156.

69. Watkins, John Pierce, "The Hero in Sir Thomas Malory," *Dissertation Abstracts*, XXVI (1965–66), 1637 (University of Pittsburgh).

An investigation of seven of Malory's knights as examples of the different kinds of heroism which exist in *Le Morte Darthur*.

70. Wilson, R. H. "Characterization in Malory: A Comparison with His Sources," Ph.D. dissertation, University of Chicago Libraries, 1934.

71. ———. "Malory's Naming of Minor Characters," *Journal of English and Germanic Philology*, XLII (1943), 364–85.

Shows that while Malory's sources usually omit proper names, Malory introduces names for these anonymous characters. Numerical evidence suggests that this tendency is not the result of accident. Long appendix listing names and where they occur in the narrative.

72. ———. "*Malory in the Connecticut Yankee*," *Studies in English*, XXVII (1948), 185–206.

Shows that most of the medieval detail in Mark Twain's book comes from Malory and that it was Mark Twain's intention to make *Le Morte Darthur* appear ludicrous.

73. ———. "How Many Books Did Malory Write?" *University of Texas Studies in English*, XXX (1951), 1–23.

Deals with the question of unity. The word *tale* had two meanings for Malory: it indicated the divisions which occurred when he changed sources; it also applied to the divisions within a part of a narrative derived from a single source, e.g., the Balin story in "The Tale of Arthur." Argues for partial unity of the book because he thinks Malory devised his plan as he went along.

74. ———. "Some Minor Characters in the *Morte Arthure*," *Modern Language Notes*, LXXI (1956), 475–80.

Uses Malory's "Tale of Arthur and Lucius" and the alliterative *Morte Arthure* to set forth principles and problems of character identification in Arthurian literature.

75. ———. "Addenda on Malory's Minor Characters," *Journal of English and Germanic Philology*, LV (1956), 563–87.

Appendix gives revised list of names apparently original to Malory in the light of new materials. Generalizes about the increased interest and unity of the narrative which results from Malory's addition of proper names.

IV. SPECIFIC STUDIES

A. Individual Tales

1. Ackerman, Robert W. "Malory's Ironsyde," *Research Studies* (Washington State University), XXXII (1964), 125–33.

Examines the Tale of Gareth and its sources by tracing reference to Sir Ironsyde, the Red Knight of the Red Lands in other romances. Ackerman rejects the theory that the Tale of Gareth is original with Malory and proposes a lost romance probably written in English as Malory's source.

2. Angelescue, Victor. "The Relationship of Gareth and Gawain in Malory's *Morte Darthur*," *Notes and Queries*, VIII (1961), 8–9.

Finds evidence that Malory has deliberately shaped the Gareth-Gawain relationship in the Tale of Gareth to foreshadow events in later tales. This information is offered in support of the single book theory.

3. Arnold, Ivor D. O. "Malory's Story of Arthur's Roman Campaign," *Medium Aevum*, VII (1938), 74–75.

Uses Malory to explore the question of whether Wace translated Geoffrey or used a lost French version of Geoffrey.

4. Dichmann, M. E. "Characterization in Malory's *Tale of Arthur and Lucius*," *Publications of the Modern Language Association*, LXV (1950), 877–95.

Accepts Vinaver's suggestion that the Tale of Arthur and Lucius may have been the first tale that Malory wrote, but nevertheless finds a great deal of evidence that the tale was not constructed as a separate romance. The body of the article compares Tale II with its source, the alliterative *Morte Arthure*, to show Malory reshaping the characters he found in his source to make them fit the roles he had designed for them in later episodes. Much of the argument also refutes Vinaver's opinion that Malory was ignorant of the French Vulgate cycles when he composed this tale.

5. Dichmann, Mary E. " 'The Tale of King Arthur and the Emperor Lucius': The Rise of Lancelot," in *Malory's Originality*, ed. R. M. Lumiansky. Baltimore, 1964. Pp. 67–90.

A slightly revised version of "Characterization in Malory's Tale of Arthur and Lucius," *Publications of the Modern Language Association*, LXV (1950), 877–95.
6. Donner, Morton. "The Backgrounds of Malory's *Book of Gareth*," *Dissertation Abstracts*, XVI (1956), 1249–50 (Columbia).

Examines the Celtic backgrounds for the Gareth story with particular emphasis on the Sickbed of Cuchulain, a ninth-century Irish tale.
7. Doskow, George. "Contrasting Narrative Forms in the Works of Thomas Malory: A Critical Study of *The Tale of King Arthur* and the *Death of King Arthur*," *Dissertation Abstracts*, XXVI (1965–66), 6694–95 (Connecticut).

Shows that Tale I is characterized by a strictly "medieval" narrative structure where causality and coherence are of no importance. Tale VIII on the other hand demonstrates a "purpose and direction" which contrast sharply with the narrative structure of Tale I.
8. Fox, M. D. "Malory and the Piteous History of the Morte Arthure," *Arthuriana*, I (1928), 30–36.

Concerned with Malory's version of the final tragedy in Books XVIII, XX, and XXI of *Le Morte Darthur*. Proposes a lost source for the incidents not found in either the stanzaic *Morte* or the prose *Mort Artu*. In the treatment of the characters Malory is less interested in their personalities than he is in their actions, and in the case of Arthur he comes close to a "ludicrous" portrait of a king so bent on reconciliation. As for Malory's contribution to the story, his most important achievement is "the identification of towns."
9. Guerin, Wilfred L. "The Function of 'The Death of Arthur' in Malory's Tragedy of the Round Table." *Dissertation Abstracts*, XIX (1958–59), 2089 (Tulane).

Finds that the tragedy of Tale VIII is dependent upon the development of the ideals of the first seven tales and is therefore the appropriate conclusion to the entire book. Malory's tragedy is not unrelieved as he has provided his principal characters with a "spiritual catharsis."
10. ———. " 'The Tale of Gareth': The Chivalric Flowering," in *Malory's Originality*, ed. R. M. Lumiansky. Baltimore, 1964. Pp. 99–117.

Allows Malory a greater measure of originality for the creation of this tale than earlier critics. The point of the tale is to give a picture of the Round Table at the height of its success and to prepare the way for Gareth's part in the final tragedy. The tale also functions as an exposition on passionate and ideal love—a theme relevant to the last three tales.

11. ———. " 'The Tale of the Death of Arthur': Catastrophe and Resolution," in *Malory's Originality*, ed. R. M. Lumiansky. Baltimore, 1964. Pp. 233–74.

Uses source comparison to show Malory choosing carefully from the stanzaic *Le Morte Arthure* and the French *Mort Artu* to produce the tragic effect he desired. Guerin sees the conclusion of the book as positive and reassuring although tragic.

12. Hibbard, L. A. "Malory's Book of Balin," in *Medieval Studies in Memory of G. S. Loomis*. New York, 1927. Pp. 175–95.

A very good essay defending Malory's version of the Balin story as more artful and significant than the version in the *Huth Merlin*. Miss Hibbard takes issue with critics who assume that Malory's drastic reduction of the story implies a lack of understanding of its meaning. The article works to show that just the opposite is true; Malory has sharpened the emphasis of the story by eliminating much of the extraneous romance material.

13. Loomis, R. S. "Malory's Beaumains," *Publications of the Modern Language Association*, LIV (1939), 656–68.

Takes issue with Vinaver's view that Malory composed certain parts of the Gareth section and modelled them on his patron Richard Beauchamp, Earl of Warwick. Shows the implausibility of the historical parallel, and also rejects the likelihood of Malory's composition of anything original except for passages of moralizing. Traces Celtic origin of the name and the history of its appearance in early Arthurian material.

14. Loomis, R. S. "The Structure of Malory's Gareth," in *Studies in Language and Literature in Honor of Margaret Schlauch*. Warsaw, 1966. Pp. 219–25.

Loomis uses the example of Malory's "Tale of Gareth" to demonstrate that the structure of medieval narrative can best be understood through a knowledge of the narrator's sources. He assumes that the tale is not original with Malory; the sources which he proposes are those of early Irish and Welsh sagas.

15. Lumiansky, R. M. "The Relationship of Lancelot and Guenevere in Malory's 'Tale of Lancelot,' " *Modern Language Notes*, LXVIII (1953), 86–91.

Function of the tale in the larger framework of the whole narrative: it establishes Lancelot as the central hero of the whole book; it exposes the relationship of Lancelot and Guenevere prior to the adultery. Shows numerous additions and changes in Malory's tale which demonstrate the unity of the entire book.

16. ———. "Malory's 'Tale of Lancelot and Guenevere' as Suspense," *Medieval Studies*, XIX (1957), 108–22.

Sets the tale against its sources to show that Malory used his materials and added to them to create suspense. The five structural subdivisions of the tale all follow the same pattern of crisis and resolution and therefore provide an ironic prologue to the series of crises in the last tale which have no satisfactory resolution.

17. ———. "Arthur's Final Companions in Malory's *Morte Darthur*," *Tulane Studies in English*, XI (1961), 5–19.

Briefly examines the chief accounts of the passing of Arthur. Malory's version depends on the stanzaic *Morte* with some minor variations; but Malory was bothered by the discrepancy between the two accounts of Arthur's death which he found in his source, and consequently tried to reconcile them with the inscription from the alliterative *Morte*. The four queens who accompany Arthur to Avalon in Malory's story represent the forces of good and evil in the world and are thematically related to the rest of the narrative.

18. ———. " 'The Tale of Lancelot': Prelude to Adultery," in *Malory's Originality*, ed. R. M. Lumiansky. Baltimore, 1964. Pp. 91–98.

A slightly revised version of "The Relationship of Lancelot and Guenevere in Malory's 'Tale of Lancelot,' " *Modern Language Notes*, LXVIII (1953), 86–91.

19. ———. " 'The Tale of Lancelot and Guenevere': Suspense," in *Malory's Originality*, ed. R. M. Lumiansky. Baltimore, 1964. Pp. 205–32.

A somewhat revised version of "Malory's 'Tale of Lancelot and Guenevere' as Suspense," *Mediaeval Studies*, XIX (1957), 108–22.

20. Moorman, Charles. "Malory's Treatment of the Sankgreall," *Publications of the Modern Language Association*, LXXI (1956), 496–509.

Examines the changes which Malory made from his source to show that Malory took great care to connect the Grail section with the themes and narrative of the whole book. For Malory the Grail symbolized the failure of Arthurian civilization, and Moorman shows how Malory sharpened the religious message of his source to make this point.

21. ———. "The Relation of Books I and III of Malory's Morte Darthur," *Mediaeval Studies* (Toronto), XXII (1960), 361–66.

Sets up a chart to show that Books I and III are purposely arranged to contrast the "old brutality and immorality" with the "New Chivalry" of the Round Table.

22. ———. " 'The Tale of the Sankgreall': Human Frailty," in *Malory's Originality*, ed. R. M. Lumiansky. Baltimore, 1964. Pp. 184–204.

Revised from "Malory's Treatment of the Sankgreall," *Publications of the Modern Language Association*, LXXI (1956), 496–509.

23. Rumble, Thomas C. " 'The Tale of Tristram': Development by Analogy," in *Malory's Originality*, ed. R. M. Lumiansky. Baltimore, 1964. Pp. 118–83.

Notes Malory's attention to the kind of cause and effect which is necessary to tragedy. The Tristram section underlines the causes of the tragedy because it functions as an analogy to the main action of the narrative. This lengthy tale also allows room for the development of the discrepancy between the ideals and the reality of Arthurian society.

24. ———. "Malory's *Balin* and the Question of Unity in the *Morte Darthur*," *Speculum*, XLI (1966), 68–85.

An effort to explain the seeming isolation of the Balin story from the rest of the narrative. Argues that the passages which introduce and conclude the story do not corroborate the separate romance theory; they are in fact evidence of a unified plan. The structural and thematic ties with the rest of Malory's work are carefully worked out to show the dependence of the narrative on the story of Balin.

25. Schueler, Donald G. "The Tristram Section of Malory's *Morte Darthur*," *Studies in Philology*, LXV (1968), 51–66.

Studies Tristram as an analogue to Lancelot and decides that Malory uses this parallelism to show that the great knight achieves significance by attaching himself to a larger structure as Lancelot does with the Round Table.

26. Tucker, P. E. "The Place of the 'Quest of the Holy Grail' in the 'Morte Darthur,' " *Modern Language Review*, XLVIII (1953), 391–97.

Points out that Malory has softened the condemnation of earthly chivalry which he found in his source by making a distinction between 'good' and 'bad' chivalry. According to Tucker, Malory attempts to reconcile the ideals of the Quest with "knyghtly dedys and vertuous lyvyng," but retains the censure of courtly love.

27. Vorontzoff, T. "Malory's Story of Arthur's Roman Campaign,"

Medium Aevum, VI (1937), 99–121. [Reply by I. D. O. Arnold, VII, 1938.]

Summarizes the differences between Caxton and the Winchester manuscript in Tale II. Shows that Winchester cannot have been the source for Caxton's edition, and traces genealogy of the story all the way from Geoffrey of Monmouth to Caxton.

28. Whitehead, F. "On Certain Episodes in the Fourth Book of Malory's Morte Darthur," *Medium Aevum*, II (1933), 199–216.

I. The Story of Pelleas and Ettard

II. The last five chapters of Book IV

Whitehead uses Malory's alterations of his source in the first episode to show that Malory did not understand the conventions of courtly love. He regards the last five chapters of Book IV as Malory's very free treatment of a late cyclic romance, and attempts to use the chapters to reveal something about Malory's "severely practical" temperament.

29. Williams, C. "Malory and the Grail Legend," *Dublin Review*, XVII (1944), 144–53.

Recognizes three degrees of love in the three Grail knights, Galahad, Percival and Bors, and notes that their ends are appropriate to their degree. "The High Prince as at the deep centre, and the others move towards him, but also he operates in them towards the world."

30. Wilson, R. H. "The 'Fair Unknown' in Malory," *Publications of the Modern Language Association*, LVIII (1943), 2–21.

A discussion of the sources of Malory's Gareth. Discards Vinaver's suggestion that Malory's source was the story of Gaheinet in the prose *Lancelot*. Traces parallels between "Gareth" and certain *Bel Inconnu* stories and decides that they and the *La Cote Male Taile* were Malory's sources for Gareth.

31. Wright, T. L. " 'The Tale of King Arthur': Beginnings and Foreshadowings," in *Malory's Originality*, ed. R. M. Lumiansky. Baltimore, 1964. Pp. 9–66.

Compares Malory's tale with its source the *Suite du Merlin* and shows that Malory has constructed an unprecedented interpretation of Arthurian life. The sequence of episodes and the references to time are designed to emphasize the uniqueness of this society which is centered in its code in the third subdivision. Wright believes that Book I was purposely designed as the first part of an extensive history of Arthur and his Round Table. He shows that Malory's departures from the *Suite du Merlin* deliberately emphasize a secular idealism not found in his source. Much of the essay is an elaborate refutation of Vinaver's theory of separate romances based upon the evidence of Malory's retrospective editions.

32. ―――. "Originality and Purpose in Malory's 'Tale of King Arthur,'" *Dissertation Abstracts,* XXI (1960–61), 2280–82 (Tulane).

A defense of the unity of *Le Morte Darthur.* By comparing Tale I with its source, the *Suite du Merlin,* Wright shows that Malory purposely shaped his material as an introduction to the whole history of Arthur and his Round Table.

33. Wroten, Helen I. "Malory's Tale of King Arthur and the Emperor Lucius Compared with Its Source, the Alliterative *Morte Arthure,*" Ph.D. dissertation, University of Illinois, 1950. Microfilm Abstracts, XI (1951).

A line-by-line comparison of Malory's "Tale of Arthur and Lucius" in Caxton's edition of Malory, the Winchester Manuscript, and the alliterative *Morte Arthure.* Argues for the unity of Malory's whole book.

B. Individual Characters

1. Bartholomew, Barbara Gray. "The Thematic Function of Malory's Gawain," *College English,* XXIV (1962-63), 262–67.

A consideration of the inconsistencies of Malory's Gawain as thematically useful to the author in his examination of the virtues and defects of Round Table society. "Galahad and, in a different sense, Lancelot, appear as the ideals in contrast to Gawain the actual." Gawain is simply representative of erring humanity incapable of fulfilling the demands of an "ideal" society.

2. Bennett, William K. "Sir Thomas Malory's Gawain: The Noble Villain," *West Virginia University Philological Papers* 16 (1967), 17–29.

A defense of Malory's treatment of Gawain. Argues that Gawain's repentance at the end of the book is perfectly consistent with Malory's plan.

3. Bogdanow, F. "The Character of Gawain in the Thirteenth Century Prose Romances," *Medium Aevum* XXVII (1958), 154–61.

Traces the two distinct French traditions in the characterization of Gawain to account for what the author considers the inconsistencies of Malory's Gawain.

4. Davies, R. T. "Was Pellynor Unworthy?" *Notes and Queries,* 202 (1957), 370.

Answers Vinaver's objection to Pellynor's behavior in Tale I where he passes a lady in distress who later commits suicide. Davies suggests that the lady is to blame if she did not save her own life when she might have.

5. Davis, Gilbert R. "Malory's 'Tale of Sir Lancelot' and the Question of Unity in the *Morte Darthur*," *Publications of the Michigan Academy of Science, Arts, and Letters*, XLIX (1964), 523–30.

The evidence for unity offered here is that of the continuous development of Lancelot's character throughout the whole book. Davis finds that Malory postpones events in his source which do not fit this pattern of development and adds other passages to prepare the reader for what is to come. He also believes that at the opening of the "Tale of Lancelot" the love affair is well under way.

6. Di Pasquale, Pasquale, Jr. "Malory's Guinevere: Epic Queen, Romance Heroine and Tragic Mistress," *Bucknell Review* 16, no. 2: 86–102.

Studies Malory's fusion of romance, epic, and tragedy and employs the tools of Northrup Frye to do so.

7. Guerin, Wilfred L. "The Functional Role of Gareth in Malory's *Morte Darthur*," Master's thesis, Tulane University, 1953.

8. ———. "Malory's *Morte Darthur*, Book VII," *Explicator*, XX (1961–62), Item 64.

The grammatical confusion concerning Gareth's nickname Beaumains is not significant. The name merely fits Malory's conception of the aristocratic knight's physical appearance; "his fists must be large, strong and square."

9. Lumiansky, R. M. "Tristram's First Interviews with Mark in Malory's *Morte Darthur*," *Modern Language Notes*, LXX (1955), 476–78.

Corrects Vinaver's reading of passage describing Tristram's introduction to Mark's court. Vinaver said that Malory has Tristram reveal his identity immediately, but a closer reading shows that Mark does not know Tristram is his nephew.

10. ———. "Gawain's Miraculous Strength: Malory's Use of *Le Morte Arthur* and *Mort Artu*," *Etudes Anglaises*, X (1957), 97–108.

Shows that Malory has juggled the two accounts in his sources of the final combat between Gawain and Lancelot to suit his own thematic purposes. The effect of Malory's "selection and alteration is to emphasize the "deterioration of relationships" which underlies the whole of the last tale.

11. ———. "Two Notes on Malory's *Morte Darthur*: Sir Urry in England—Lancelot's Burial Vow," *Neophilologische Mitteilungen*, LVIII (1957), 148–53.

12. ———. "Malory's Steadfast Bors," *Tulane Studies in English*, VIII (1958), 5–20.

Traces original and borrowed references to Bors from Tale 1 on to show Malory shaping this character for the important role which he had designed for him in the last three tales. This evidence argues strongly for the theory that Malory had a unified conception of *Le Morte Darthur*.

13. Morgan, Henry Grady. "The Role of Morgan Le Fay in Malory's *Morte Darthur*," *Southern Quarterly*, II (1963–64), 150–68.

Pursues theme of disloyalty through the book and points to Malory's handling of Morgan as a symbol of this theme. Finds a parallel between "Arthur and Acolon" section and "Day of Destiny" in their disclosure of the fatal distrust which exists between relatives.

14. Newstead, Helaine. "The Besieged Ladies in Arthurian Romance," *Publications of the Modern Language Association,* LXIII (1948), 803–30.

Studies the tradition of the besieged lady story by concentrating first on Malory's *Tale of Gareth* which contains elements common to the majority of such stories. Uncovers a Celtic background for these tales.

15. Olstead, Myra. "Morgan Le Fay in Malory's *Morte Darthur*," *Bulletin Bibliographique de la Société Internationale Arthurienne*, 19 (1967), 128–38.

16. Schmidz, Cornelia C. D. "Sir Gareth of Orkeney, Studien zum Siebenten Buch von Malory's Morte Darthur." Groningen, 1963.

Comparative study of Malory's Gareth and other medieval treatments of the "fair unknown."

17. Whitehead, F. "Lancelot's Penance," in *Essays on Malory*, ed. J. A. W. Bennett. Oxford, 1963. Pp. 104–13.

Like Vinaver, Whitehead finds that Malory's *Tale of the Death of King Arthur* perverts the religious message of its French source. Lancelot's penance is not a religious gesture; it is simply the only alternative open to him after Guinevere retires from the world. While the *Mort Artu* concludes by turning away from the vanities of the world, Malory's final tale presumably demonstrates Lancelot's reluctance to abandon worldly affections.

V. SOURCE AND BACKGROUND STUDIES

1. Ackerman, Robert W. *An Index of the Arthurian Names in Middle English.* Stanford, 1952.

Does not include the chronicles, but indexes names of persons and places in Middle English versions of Arthurian legends. Besides identifying the names, variant spellings are also included, with citations of where they occur in various works and occasional speculations on their origins.

2. App, August J. *Lancelot in English Literature: His Role and Character.* Washington, D. C., 1929.

In the chapters which deal with Malory's Lancelot, App gives a very moral reading of *Le Morte Darthur.* Malory's Lancelot is at once more manly and less principled than the Lancelot of his predecessors. This apparent contradiction in characterization is a consequence of Malory's placing courtly love at the center of his romance.

3. Barbour, Richard. *Arthur of Albion.* London, 1961.

An historical account of Arthur from the medieval English chronicles and romances through to T. H. White, intended as a guide for the general reader. The section on Malory summarizes the tales and includes the usual critical commonplaces.

4. Brengle, Richard L. *Arthur, King of Britain.* New York, 1964.

An anthology of excerpts from Arthurian literature with an introduction. Not very useful.

5. Bruce, J. D. "The Middle- English Metrical Romance 'Le Morte Arthur' (Harleian MS. 2252): Its Sources and Its Relation to Sir Thomas Malory's Morte Darthur," *Anglia,* XXIII (1901), 67–100.

Bruce sets out to amend Sommer's view (Vol. III of Sommer's edition) that the last two books of *Le Morte Darthur* are a prose rendering of the metrical *Le Morte Arthur.* Instead he insists that both pieces are derived from the same French original. The lists of discrepancies between the two texts are valuable even though Bruce always assumes that when there are transpositions or additions in Malory's version they are not original but evidence of a lost source.

6. ———, ed. *"Le Morte Arthur, a Romance in Stanzas of Eight Lines,"* *Early English Text Society, English Studies, LXXXVIII* (1903), 13–20.

Introduction discusses the relationship of the stanzaic poem to Malory and summarizes the points made in the *Anglia* article (XXIII, 1901, pp. 67ff).

7. ———. *The Evolution of Arthurian Romance.* 2 vols. Baltimore, 1928.

Although Bruce never discusses Malory except in passing, his work on the sources is extremely useful.

8. Chambers, E. K. *Arthur of Britain.* London, 1927.

Only mentions Malory in passing twice but contains much

information about earlier branches of the Arthurian story.
The chapter headings are: The Early Tradition; Geoffrey of
Monmouth; the Sources of Geoffrey; Acceptance of Arthur;
Arthur and the Round Table; Historicity of Arthur; Arthur
and Mythology.

9. Donaldson, E. T. "Malory and the Stanzaic *Le Morte Arthur*,"
Studies in Philology, XLVII (1950), 460–72.

Opposes Vinaver's theory that the source of Book XVIII
(Poisoned Apple, and Maid of Astolat episodes) is the French
prose *Mort Artu* and not the English stanzaic poem *Le Morte
Arthur*. Works out the source relationship between the English poem and Malory's version to demonstrate Malory's skill
as a story teller.

10. Gibson, J. W. "The Characterization of King Arthur in Medieval English Literature," V. *Index to Theses Accepted for
Higher Degrees*, V (1954–55), 137 (Sheffield).

11. Gordon, E. V., and E. Vinaver. "New Light on the Text of the
Alliterative *Morte Arthure*," *Medium Aevum*, VI (1937), 81–98.

A thorough study of the Caxton and Winchester versions of
The Tale of Arthur and Lucius showing the extensive revisions
which Caxton made. The authors briefly outline what seem to
them to be Malory's additions to his source, but the body of the
article is devoted to reconstruction the alliterative *Morte Arthure* which Malory must have known from the evidence of the
Winchester manuscript.

12. Graves, Robert. "Kynge Arthur is Nat Dede," in *The Crown-
ing Privilege*. London, 1955. Pp. 210–15.

A brief account of the various legends surrounding the burial
place of Arthur. Graves finds that Arthur cannot be studied
as one studies the legendary heroes of Greece, Rome and France:
"The best we can do with King Arthur is to accept him as a
national obsession, and his paradoxes as peculiarly insular."

13. Griffith, R. H. "Malory, *Morte Arthure* and *Fierabras*," *Anglia*,
XXXII (1909), 389–98.

14. Housman, J. E. "Higden, Trevisa, Caxton, and the Beginnings
of Arthurian Criticism," *Review of English Studies*, XXIII
(1947), 209–17.

Defines medieval views of history and romance by looking
at three critics of the Arthurian story. Trevisa defends the
authenticity of Geoffrey of Monmouth's Arthur, but he makes
no real distinction between fact and fiction. Higden and Caxton see history as a set of moral examples which must be true
in order to fulfill their moral purpose. Consequently there is
some scepticism on the part of both Higden and Caxton con-

cerning the merits of the Arthurian story because it is based on uncertain authority.

15. Kennedy, Elspeth. "The Two Versions of the False Guinevere Episode in the Old French Prose Lancelot," *Romance Notes*, LXXXVII (1956), 94–104.

A good illustration of the expansion of a story by the method of *entrelacement*. Although Kennedy makes no mention of Malory, he gives some very useful material on the nature of Malory's French sources.

16. Loomis, L. H. "Arthur's Round Table," *Publications of the Modern Language Association*, XLI (1926), 771–84.

Does not mention Malory. Concentrates on establishing the Christian origins of the Round Table by showing that there was an unbroken tradition in religious art in Wace's Normandy which depicted Christ and the Apostles sitting at a round table for the Last Supper. As round tables were virtually unknown in daily medieval life, Mrs. Loomis concludes that Arthur's Round Table has religious origins and associations.

17. Loomis, R. S. "*Onomastic Riddles in Malory's Book of Arthur and His Knights,*" *Medium Aevum*, XXV (1956), 181–90.

Traces the genealogy of some of the names in *Le Morte Darthur* as a way of tracing the legends associated with them back to their Celtic origins.

18. ——, ed. *Arthurian Literature in the Middle Ages: A Collaborative History*. Oxford, 1959.

Forty-one articles on various aspects of Arthurian literature. Most of these pieces are relevant to the study of Malory and his sources.

19. ——. *The Development of Arthurian Romance*. New York, 1963.

Deals briefly and sceptically with the traditional biographical material. On the matter of unity, Loomis concludes that although some of the tales were conceived as separate pieces, Malory later worked them into a whole. He examines Malory's use of his sources and demonstrates the artistry of his narrative technique in this light.

20. Lot, F. *Etude sur le Lancelot en Prose*. Paris, 1918.

Chapters on the principle of *entrelacement*, chronology, unity of plan and spirit, internal contradictions, social milieu of the work, sources, literary faults and merits. Very useful background study for comparison with Malory's narrative.

21. Matthews, William. *The Tragedy of Arthur: A Study of the Alliterative "Morte Arthure."* Berkeley and Los Angeles, 1960.

Very important study of Malory's source for Tale II. Especially good on medieval notions of tragedy and their relationship to the Arthurian story.

22. Maynadier, G. H. *The Arthur of the English Poets*. Cambridge, 1907.

Comments on Malory are rather superficial. Regards *Le Morte Darthur* as a compilation of Arthurian material which is unique for its emphasis on Arthur as the central figure. Finds that the value of the book lies in its style and in the rapidity of its action.

23. McNair, W. F. "A Possible Source for the *Irish Knight*" [probably Malory], *Modern Language Notes*, LVIII (1943), 383–85.

Proposes the story of Launceor and Colombe in *Le Morte Darthur* as source for one of the lost plays presented at the Court of Queen Elizabeth referred to as "The Irisshe Knyght."

24. Moorman, Charles. "Cretien's Knights: The Uses of Love," *Southern Quarterly*, I (1963), 247–72.

Good for comparative studies—no mention of Malory.

25. ———. "King Arthur and the English National Character," *New York Folklore Quarterly*, 24 (1968), 103–12.

26. Morton, A. L. "The Matter of Britain," *Zeitschrift für Anglistik und Amerikanistik*, VIII, no. 1 (1960), 5–28.

Traces process of transformation of Arthurian story from chronicle to romance and explains this process by reference to the growth and decay of feudal society. Dwells on the political aspects of Malory's book.

27. Parsons, Coleman O. "A Scottish 'Father of Courtesy' and Malory," *Speculum*, XX (1945), 51–64.

Finds similarities between the famous fight at Gasklune in 1312 and King Arthur's last battle in *Le Morte Darthur*. Finds it probable that Malory would have been interested in the "ornament" of Scottish chivalry embodied in the life of Sir David Lindsay.

28. Reid, Margaret C. J. *The Arthurian Legend in Modern Literature*. Edinburgh, 1938.

    I. Comparison of courtly love in Marie de France, Cretien, and Malory; medieval and modern treatments compared.

    II. Arthur in the Chronicles and in Malory.

    VII. Lancelot in Cretien, Malory and later writers.

    VIII. The Welsh tradition—some comments on Malory.

    IX. Early versions of the Grail including Malory.

    XIII. Tristan: Sources and Malory.

    XVI. Satire, Dinaden in Malory.

Uses Malory throughout as "landmark" between medieval and
modern treatments of the Arthurian legend.
29. Rumble, Thomas C. "The Tristram Legend and its Place in the
Morte Darthur," Ph.D. dissertation, Tulane University, 1955.
30. Ryding, William Wellington. "Structural Patterns in Medieval
Narrative," *Dissertation Abstracts*, XXVI (1965–66), 3308–9
(Columbia).
Primarily concerned with Old French literature with brief
mention of Malory.
31. Saintsbury, G. *The Flourishing of Romance and the Rise of
Allegory*. New York, 1897.
Mentions Malory only briefly and cautions readers against
considering him merely as a compiler. Finds that Malory's
omissions as well as the things which he includes demonstrate a
sharp sense of literary fitness. Treats materials which formed
some of Malory's sources in depth.
32. Scudder, Vida D. *Le Morte Darthur of Sir Thomas Malory and
Its Sources*. New York, 1921.
Part I "Malory's Predecessors," a study of both French and
English romances as well as chronicles; Part II, "Malory's
Morte Darthur," biographical material plus a thematic analysis
of the book; Part III, "Malory and His Sources," a study of
Malory's borrowings, revisions, and additions. Miss Scudder
is very good in her analysis of the genres of romance and
chronicle as they affect Malory's composition.
33. Stephens, G. Arbour. *Mallory's Land of Goire or House of
Most Worship*. Aberystwyth, 1933.
34. Ten Bensel, Elise van der Ven. *The Character of King Arthur
in English Literature*. Amsterdam, 1925.
Traces the various representations of King Arthur from
early chronicle to Tennyson. Finds that Malory begins to develop Arthur's character by presenting him as more virtuous
in later life, but falls short of a consistent psychological por-
traiture.
35. Tucker, P. E. "A Source for 'The Healing of Sir Urry' in the
'Morte Darthur,'" *Modern Language Review*, L (1955), 490–92.
Finds an earlier version of Malory's Sir Urry episode in the
French *Prose Lancelot*.
36. Vinaver, Eugene. *Le Roman de Tristan et Iseult dans l'Oeuvre
de Thomas Malory*. Paris, 1925.
Considers Malory's Tristan as an important part of the
extant Tristan legends. Examines its sources and uses them as
a basis for commenting on Malory's version of the story. Includes some very valuable analyses of Malory's narrative methods

but concludes by relegating Malory to the status of "intermediare entre deux langues et deux civilisations."

37. ———. "Notes on Malory's Sources," *Arthuriana*, I (1928), 64–66.

The first note provides a piece of evidence to prove that Malory's source for Book XVIII was French. Note 2 shows that the Huth MS of the Merlin is the closest extant text to Malory's source for his account of Merlin.

38. ———. "A Romance of Gaheret," *Medium Aevum*, I (1932), 157–67.

Vinaver proposes a lost source for Malory's "Tale of Gareth" and for many other romances which concern the "fair unknown."

39. ———. "The Legend of Wade in the Morte Darthur," *Medium Aevum*, II (1933), 135–36.

An example of Malory remembering a line from the alliterative *Morte Arthure* referring to Wade's adventures and including it in the speech of Lady Linet, Bk. VII, Ch. IX.

40. ———. "La Genèse de la *Suite du Merlin*," in *Melanges de philologie Romane et de littérature médiévale offerts à Ernest Hoepffner*. Publication de la Faculté des lettres et de l'Université de Strasbourg. Paris, 1949.

41. Wilson, R. H. "Malory and the Perlesvaus," *Modern Philology*, XXX (1932), 13–22.

Finds a parallel in Malory's "Tale of Lancelot" between Chapters XIV–XV and an episode in the French prose romance *Perlesvaus*. Lists all the parallel passages and suggests that the *Perlesvaus* may be a good point from which the scholar can examine Malory's originality.

42. ———. "Malory, the Stanzaic *Morte Arthur* and the *Mort Artu*," *Modern Philology*, XXXVII (1939), 125–38.

Discusses the question of Malory's indebtedness to the *Mort Artu* or the stanzaic *Morte Arthur* for Books XVIII, XX, XXI. Favors view that Malory used both sources. Admits that although Malory sticks closely to his sources, he is capable of making changes which serve a specific purpose.

43. ———. "Malory's 'French Book' Again," *Comparative Literature*, II (1950), 172–81.

Collects all of Malory's references to his "French Book" to show that "the book" is used to indicate Malory's source at the moment of writing. "There is no implication that the French book is always the same one."

44. ———. "Malory's Early Knowledge of Arthurian Romance," *University of Texas Studies in English*, XXIX (1950).

Finds evidence that Malory knew more about Arthurian ro-

mance and especially the character of Lancelot than what appeared in the sources he was retelling. Isolates some of Malory's sourceless statements about Tristram and Lancelot and
points to characters that Malory uses which are not in his
sources. Wilson's article is written partly as a response to
Vinaver's theory that Malory knew nothing of the Vulgate
cycle when he began to write.

45. ———. "Notes on Malory's Sources," *Modern Language Notes,*
LXVI (1951), 22–26.

Written in reply to some of Vinaver's statements about Malory's use of source materials. Wilson tends to discount theories
which involve reconstructing lost sources. Malory may have
written from memory which would account for the variations
between his versions and those of his sources; he need not
always have translated directly.

46. ———. "The Rebellion of the Kings in Malory and in the
Cambridge *Suite du Merlin,*" *University of Texas Studies in
English,* XXXI (1952), 13–26.

The Cambridge *Suite* represents the kind of source Malory
must have used for the episode of the Rebellion since the
Huth manuscript does not contain the episode at all. Article
explores source relationship as evidence of medieval redactors
"working with originality and ingenuity."

47. ———. "The Prose *Lancelot* in Malory," *University of Texas
Studies in English,* XXXII (1953), 1–13.

The major departures from the source in Tale III may be the
result of Malory's using a modified version of the prose *Lancelot* although Wilson gives good evidence that Malory made the
changes himself. Shows that variant details in Tale VII are
the result of the author writing from memory of sources read
sometime earlier.

VI. BIOGRAPHY

1. Altick, Richard D. "The Quest of the Knight Prisoner," *The
Scholar Adventurers.* New York, 1950. Pp. 65–85.

An account of all the major attempts to identify the author
of *Le Morte Darthur,* plus an interpretation of Malory's literary
intentions based on the recently discovered Winchester manuscript. Altick's views are conditioned by his acceptance of
Kittredge's identification of Malory and upon his agreement
with Vinaver that Malory wrote eight separate romances.

2. Aurner, N. S., ed. *Malory: An Introduction to the "Morte Darthur."* New York, 1938.

The introduction to these selections from Malory contains biographical information concerning Richard Beauchamp, Earl of Warwick, and the Duke of Buckingham, and of course some speculation about the career of the author and its supposed relationship to these two figures. The rest of the introduction is devoted to the question of "Malory's book as a reflection of his life."

3. Baugh, A. C. "Documenting Malory," *Speculum*, VIII (1933), 3–29.

A summary of the biographical research of Kittredge, Hicks and others which accepts Kittredge's identification of Malory as the "Sir Thomas Malory, Knight of Wimwick (Northhamptonshire) and Newbold Revell (Warwickshire)" and proceeds to an examination of this man's criminal record.

4. Hicks, E. *Sir Thomas Malory, His Turbulent Career: A Biography.* Cambridge, Mass., 1928.

Hicks accepts Kittredge's identification of the author of *Le Morte Darthur* with the Sir Thomas Malory of Newbold Revell, Warwickshire. His own additions to the biography of this man are drawn from his researches in the Public Record Office. Although the recent biographical study of Malory by William Matthews (*The Ill-Framed Knight*, Berkeley, 1966) has virtually destroyed Kittredge's theory of Malory's identity, Hicks's book nevertheless contains much valuable material on Malory's times. The brief analysis of *Le Morte Darthur* rests on Hicks's shaky biographical assumptions and is less useful.

5. Kittredge, G. L. *Who Was Sir Thomas Malory?* Boston, 1897. [Reprinted from *Studies and Notes in Philology and Literature*, Vol. V, pp. 85–106].

Kittredge's famous identification of the knight-prisoner.

6. Martin, A. T. "Sir Thomas Malory," *Athenaeum* (1897), pp. 353–54.

Discusses the Pappeworth will of 1469 which he attributes to the Sir Thomas Malory who wrote *Le Morte Darthur*.

7. ———. "The Identity of the Author of the Morte Darthur," *Archaeologia*, LVI (1898), 165–77.

A genealogical inquiry into the family to "two" Sir Thomas Malorys which attempts to prove that they are the same man. Concludes that the author of *Le Morte Darthur* was born on the border of Wales and died in 1469 after serving on the Lancastrian side in the Wars of the Roses.

8. Matthews, William. *The Ill-Framed Knight: A Skeptical Inquiry into the Identity of Sir Thomas Malory.* Berkeley, 1966.

A study which has virtually invalidated all the earlier scholarship on Malory's biography. Matthews destroys the cases for each of the three Sir Thomas Malorys who have been proposed as the authors of *Le Morte Darthur*. Using the evidence of dialect, probable age, and career, Matthews proposes an entirely new candidate whose political sympathies and moral character do not present as many paradoxes as the Sir Thomas Malory of Newbold Revell proposed by Kittredge.

9. Williams, T. W. Letter to the *Athenaeum,* No. 3585 (July 11, 1896), pp. 64–65.

This letter announces the discovery of a general pardon dated August 24, 1468, under the seal of King Henry IV which excluded a "Thomas Malory, miles."

Bibliography

AUERBACH, ERICH. *Literary Language and Its Public in the Later Middle Ages*. New York: Pantheon Books, 1965.

———. *Mimesis*. New York: Anchor Books, 1957.

AURNER, N. S. "Sir Thomas Malory—Historian?" *Publications of the Modern Language Association*, XLVIII (1933), 362–91.

BREWER, D. S. "Form in the Morte Darthur," *Medium Aevum*, XXI (1952), 14–24.

———. " 'The hoole book,' " *Essays on Malory*, edited by J. A. W. Bennett. Oxford: Oxford University Press, 1963. Pp. 41–63.

BRUCE, J. D. "The Middle-English Metrical Romance 'Le Morte Arthur' (Harleian MS 2252): Its Sources and Its Relation to Sir Thomas Malory's Morte Darthur," *Anglia*, XXIII (1901), 67–100.

COOKSEY, C. F. "The Morte D'Arthur," *Nineteenth Century* (June, 1924), 852–59.

DE ROUGEMONT, DENIS. *Love in the Western World*. New York: Fawcett Publications, 1940.

DICKINSON, JOHN. "The Medieval Conception of Kingship as Developed in the *Policraticus* of John of Salisbury," *Speculum*, I (1926), 307–37.

FERGUSON, ARTHUR B. *The Indian Summer of English Chivalry:*

Studies in the Decline and Transformation of Chivalric Idealism. Durtham, N.C.: Duke University Press, 1960.

FORTESCUE, SIR JOHN. *De Laudibus Legum Angliae.* Translated by Francis Gregor. London: Sweet and Maxwell, Ltd., 1917.

GEOFFREY OF MONMOUTH. *History of the Kings of Britain.* Translated by Sebastian Evans. New York: E. P. Dutton & Co., 1958.

HANNING, ROBERT W. *The Vision of History in Early Britain.* New York: Columbia University Press, 1966.

HARTMAN, GEOFFREY. "Structuralism: The Anglo-American Adventure," *Yale French Studies,* 36 and 37 (1966), 148–69.

HENRY OF BRACTON. *De legibus et consuetudinibus Angliae,* edited by G. E. Woodbine. New Haven: Yale University Press, 1922.

HUIZINGA, JOHAN. *Men and Ideas.* New York: Meridian Books, 1959.

JOHN OF SALISBURY. *Policraticus,* edited by C. J. Webb. Oxford: Clarendon Press, 1909.

KANTOROWICZ, ERNST. *The King's Two Bodies: A Study in Mediaeval Political Theology.* Princeton: Princeton University Press, 1957.

KEELER, LAURA. "Geoffrey of Monmouth and the Late Latin Chroniclers," *University of California Publications in English,* XVII, no. 1 (1946).

LÉVI-STRAUSS, CLAUDE. *Structural Anthropology.* New York: Anchor Books, 1967.

LOOMIS, LAURA H. "Arthur's Round Table," *Publications of the Modern Language Association,* XLI (1926), 771–84.

LUMIANSKY, R. M. "The Alliterative *Morte Arthure*: The Concept of Medieval Tragedy, and the Cardinal Virtue of Fortitude," *Medieval and Renaissance Studies,* III (1968), 95-118.

———. "Gawain's Miraculous Strength: Malory's Use of *Le Morte Arthur* and *Mort Artu,*" Etudes Anglaises, X (1957), 97–108.

———. "Malory's Steadfast Bors," *Tulane Studies in English,* VIII (1958), 5–25.

———. "The Question of Unity in Malory's *Morte Darthur,*" *Tulane Studies in English,* V (1955), 29–39.

———. "The Relationship of Lancelot and Guenevere in Malory's 'Tale of Lancelot,'" *Modern Language Notes,* LXVIII (1953), 86–91.

———. "The Tale of Lancelot and Guenevere," in *Malory's Originality,* edited by R. M. Lumiansky. Baltimore: Johns Hopkins Press, 1964.

MATTHEWS, WILLIAM. *The Ill-Framed Knight.* Berkeley: University of California Press, 1966.

MOORMAN, CHARLES. *The Book of Kyng Arthur: The Unity of Malory's Morte Darthur.* Lexington: University of Kentucky Press, 1965.

————. "Internal Chronology in Malory's Morte Darthur," *Journal of English and Germanic Philology,* LX (1961), 240–49.

————. *A Knyght There Was.* Lexington: University of Kentucky Press, 1967.

————. "Lot and Pellinore: The Failure of Loyalty in Malory's 'Morte Darthur,'" *Mediaeval Studies,* XXV (1963), 83–92.

————. "Malory's Tragic Knights," *Mediaeval Studies,* XXVII (1965), 117–27.

MORTON, A. L. "The Matter of Britain," *Zeitschrift für Anglistik und Amerikanistik,* VIII, no. 1 (1960), 5–28.

POULET, GEORGES. *Studies in Human Time.* New York: Harper Torchbooks, 1956.

REISS, EDMUND. *Sir Thomas Malory.* New York: Twayne Publishers, 1966.

RUMBLE, THOMAS C. "The First *Explicit* in Malory's *Morte Darthur,*" *Modern Language Notes,* LXXI (1956), 564–66.

————. " 'The Tale of Tristram': Development by Analogy," in *Malory's Originality,* edited by R. M. Lumiansky. Baltimore: Johns Hopkins Press, 1964. Pp. 118–83.

SCHLAUCH, MARGARET. *English Medieval Literature and Its Social Foundations.* Warsaw: Państwowe Wydawnictwo Nankowe, 1956.

SCHOFIELD, W. H. *Chivalry in English Literature.* Cambridge, Mass.: Harvard University Press, 1912.

SCHRAMM, PERCY E. *A History of the English Coronation Oath.* Oxford: Clarendon Press, 1937.

SCHULZ, FRITZ. "Bracton on Kingship," *English Historical Review,* LX (1945), 136–76.

SCUDDER, VIDA. *Le Morte Darthur of Sir Thomas Malory and Its Sources.* New York: E. P. Dutton & Co., 1921.

SOMMER, H. OSKAR, ed. *The Vulgate Version of the Arthurian Romances.* Washington, D. C.: Carnegie Institution, 1913.

TUCKER, P. E. "The Place of the 'Quest of the Holy Grail' in the 'Morte Darthur,'" *Modern Language Review,* XLVIII (1953), 391–97.

TUVE, ROSEMOND. *Allegorical Imagery: Some Medieval Books and Their Posterity.* Princeton: Princeton University Press, 1966.

————. *Seasons and Months: Studies in a Tradition of Middle English Poetry.* Paris: Librairie Universitaire, 1933.

ULLMANN, W. "Influence of John of Salisbury," *English Historical Review,* LIX (1944), 384ff.

VINAVER, EUGENE, ed. *The Works of Sir Thomas Malory.* 3 vols. Oxford: Clarendon Press, 1947.

————. *The Works of Sir Thomas Malory.* Oxford: Oxford University Press, 1954.

WILSON, R. H. "How Many Books Did Malory Write?" *University of Texas Studies in English,* XXX (1951), 1–23.

————. "Malory's Naming of Minor Characters," *Journal of English and Germanic Philology,* XLII (1943), 364-85.

WRIGHT, T. L. "'The Tale of King Arthur: Beginnings and Foreshadowings," in *Malory's Originality,* edited by R. M. Lumiansky. Baltimore: Johns Hopkins Press, 1964. Pp. 9–66.

Index

A

Aggravayne, 111-12

Armagnac manuscript, 7, 15

Arthur, 17, 18; historicity of, 29-31; and Geoffrey, 53-54, 74-75; life parallels life of Christ, 55-56; portrayed as fifteenth-century king, 56-58, 77-88, 88-92; and Mark, 97-100; failure to distinguish between roles, 107-8, 111, 124, 132-40; neglect of spiritual purpose, 110, 115; loss of trust in, 123-25, 127, 132-40; and the Arthur of French romances, 77-88, 130-31

Auerbach, Erich, 70, 76-77, 108

Augustine, Augustinian, 38, 59

B

Balin, 8, 17, 62-65, 75, 81-82, 101, 105, 118

Bedwer, 137-38

Bennett, J. A. W., 4n

Bors, 90, 97, 118, 121-23, 124

B

Bracton, Henry of, 36, 43-46, 49, 51, 83, 99

Brewer, D. S., 12, 14

Bruce, J. D., 7-8

C

Caxton, William, 6n, 20-21, 34, 108

Chaucer, Geoffrey, 5, 23

Chrétien de Troyes, xii

Cooksey, C. F., 3n

D

de Rougemont, Denis, 24, 113-14

Dickinson, John, 41n

Dinaden, 18, 111-14

E

Edward II, 47-48

F

Ferguson, Arthur, 20, 28

Fortescue, Sir John, 32, 43, 45, 47-53, 55, 57, 67, 75, 84, 86-87, 96-101